JN085371

A Bilingual Introduction to
Financial Accounting

対訳 英語で学ぶ

財務会計入門

本合暁詩
Akashi Hongo

中央経済社

Preface

Welcome to Financial Accounting. Anyone who grabs this book must be interested in learning financial accounting, particularly someone who has a specific interest in learning it in ENGLISH.

Recently, Japanese universities have increased the number of lectures taught in English so that students may learn a language and the content of the lecture simultaneously.

Financial accounting is often learned in the relatively early stages among business-related subjects, and there are many accounting-specific technical terminologies which demand tremendous effort to understand them in a non-native language.

In addition, English-speaking students from outside Japan often express the desire to work in Japan after graduating from university, so it is helpful to study financial accounting in both languages.

In order to meet these needs, this book deploys English on the left page and Japanese on the right page, resulting in a comprehensive bilingual textbook to introduce financial accounting.

On a side note, the textbooks with the same format, "Bilingual Introduction to Corporate Finance (1st and 2nd edition)" and "Bilingual Introduction to Valuation" are used as a designated text for the courses the author lectures at Showa Women's University, Temple University, Rikkyo University, and Hosei University. As planned, these textbooks are received well by Japanese students who take lectures in English, and are also popular with non Japanese students who want to study Japanese and business at the same time.

The financial accounting course I am in charge of teaches accounting as the knowledge necessary to run any business. This book focuses on accounting knowledge as a practical tool that is required by every business person, instead of accounting to become an accountant.

はじめに

　財務会計へようこそ。本書を手にしている方は，財務会計を学びたいと考えている，特に英語で Financial Accounting を学ぶことに興味を持っている方でしょう。

　昨今，日本の大学において英語で行われる講義が増加しており，講義のコンテンツと同時に言語の習得が求められるケースが増えています。

　財務会計はビジネス関連科目の中でも比較的初期の段階で学ぶことが多いにもかかわらず，会計特有の専門用語が数多く存在します。これを母国語ではない言語で理解することは大変な努力を要します。

　加えて，英語が母国語または英語を得意とする海外からの学生も，大学卒業後に日本で働きたいと考えていることが多く，財務会計を英語だけではなく日本語でも学びたいと言います。

　本書は，こうしたニーズにこたえるために用意された，見開きの左ページに英語を，右ページに日本語を記載した完全日本語英語併記の財務会計入門の教科書です。

　ちなみに，本書と同様の仕様の『対訳　英語で学ぶコーポレートファイナンス入門（初版，第 2 版）』および『対訳　英語で学ぶバリュエーション入門』は，著者が英語で講義を行う，昭和女子大学，テンプル大学，立教大学，および法政大学でも指定テキストとして活用しており，出版時の想定どおり，英語で講義を受ける日本人学生から良好な評判を得ていることに加え，ビジネス知識と同時に日本語を学びたいという海外からの留学生にも好評です。

　現在私が担当している財務会計のクラスは，ビジネスを行うために必要な知識としての会計を教えています。本書でも，会計士になるための会計ではなく，あくまでビジネスパーソンとして必要となる実用的なツールとしての会計知識に焦点を当てています。

Chapter 1 overviews the basic concepts of accounting and the structure of the accounting system. This includes understanding the meaning and components of financial statements, such as balance sheets, income statements, and cash flow statements. Chapter 2 explains how each business activity, such as financing, purchasing, employing, and selling, is recorded in standard financial statements by following along with a business case study. Throughout the case, we will observe how the accounting items change, and how these changes affect all of the financial statements. Chapter 3 discusses the financial analysis methods for interpreting financial information and how each of the financial statements is interrelated by utilizing actual accounting procedures. Recent accounting topics will also be introduced in this chapter.

Despite packing two books worth of content compactly, this book covers sufficient topics and will adequately work as an introduction textbook for undergraduate/ graduate students but also as a robust reference for business professionals who are seeking financial accounting knowledge.

There are many books related to accounting, such as textbooks, practical books, and qualification exam preparation books. There are also books that provide summaries and glossaries in English to outline accounting. However, a book that explains the basics of accounting in both Japanese and English in full translation with story tailoring hardly exists. This book is designed to be completed as one book that teaches the basics of accounting and the other language simultaneously for both native Japanese speakers and native English speakers. **This book allows you to get a primer on financial accounting in Japanese and English at the same time.**

Now, let's begin the lecture.

第1章では，会計の基本的な概念と会計システムの構造を学びます。貸借対照表，損益計算書，キャッシュフロー計算書といった財務諸表の意味と構成要素の理解もここに含まれます。次の第2章では，ストーリーに沿って資金を調達する，物品を購入する，従業員を雇用する，商品を販売する，といった1つひとつの事業活動がどのように標準的な財務諸表に記録されるのかを説明していきます。この際には単に変化する会計項目だけではなく，必ず財務諸表全体の中でどこが変化するのか，そしてそれがどのように他の項目に影響するのかを観察していきます。さらに第3章では，財務諸表に記載されている情報を解釈する財務分析の手法と，財務諸表それぞれがどのように関係しているのかを実際の会計の手続きを学びながら理解していきます。最近の財務会計をめぐるトピックについてもこの章で紹介します。

　本書では日本語英語と2冊分の内容をコンパクトに詰め込んでいるわけですが，だからといって内容が薄いというわけではありません。大学生・大学院生の入門テキストとしてだけではなく，財務会計の知識が必要な社会人の方にもお使いいただける内容になっていると思います。

　会計に関連する書籍は教科書，実務書，また資格試験対策本など数多く存在します。また，英語の要約や用語集を用意して会計の概略を説明する書籍もあります。しかし，ストーリー仕立てで会計の基礎を日英両言語完全対訳で説明する書籍はこれまでなかったと思います。本書は日本語ネイティブにとっても英語ネイティブにとっても，もう一方の言語と同時に会計の基礎を学ぶ書籍として完結できることを狙っています。本書により，読者の皆さんは，この1冊で日本語と英語の財務会計の入門書を同時に手に入れることができます。

　では，さっそく講義を始めましょう。

Table of Contents

Chapter 1

Understanding Financial Statements
In what form are business activities recorded?

Chapter 2

Recording Business Activities
How do transactions change the financial statements?

第2章
事業活動の記録
取引はどのように財務三表に変化を与えるのか

Constructing and Analyzing Financial Statements
What do the financial statements represent?

Chapter 1

Understanding Financial Statements
In what form are business activities recorded?

- This chapter begins with an overview of the fundamentals of financial accounting and moves on to cover the structure and contents of the three calculation tables in which accounting information is aggregated.

- The company's main accounting information is shown in the financial statements: balance sheet, income statement, and cash flow statement.
  - The balance sheet represents a company's assets, liabilities, and shareholders' equity at a particular time.
  - The income statement shows sales, expenses, and profits over a period of time.
  - The cash flow statement represents the movement of cash over a period of time.

- The figures in these financial statements are not isolated and each figure is related to the figures in the other financial statements.

第1章

財務諸表の理解
事業活動はどのようなフォーマットに記録されるのか

★

- 本章では，まず財務会計の概略をとらえた上で，会計情報が集約される3つの計算書（表）の構造と中身を学びます。

- 企業の主な会計情報は貸借対照表，損益計算書，キャッシュフロー計算書という財務三表に示されます。

  - 貸借対照表は一時点における企業の資産，負債，資本を表わします。
  - 損益計算書は一定期間における売上高，費用，利益を示します。

  - キャッシュフロー計算書は，一定期間における現金の動きを表わします。

- これらの財務三表における数値は単独に存在するのではなく，他の財務諸表の数値と関係しあっています。

What is Accounting?

○ Accounting is a Common Language

Accounting is a system that comprehensively represents a company's business as a number. Accounting records business activities as numerical information allowing people inside and outside the company to grasp the status of business performance. Therefore, accounting is a vital mechanism when doing business, and an essential tool to understand and explain it. Accounting is the common language of businesspeople around the world.

○ What Accounting Represents

Accounting shows the monetary value of various business activities as a number. Because of this, events where the monetary value cannot be measured and transactions that do not affect the monetary value are outside the scope of accounting. In that sense, accounting does not cover all business activities.

Accounting is likened to a map. A map does not show everything in reality and is missing scenery, road signs, roadside trees, and streetscapes. However, it is certain that it is difficult to reach a destination without a map. Accounting does not represent every aspect of the business, but it is impossible to do business without accounting.

○ Financial Accounting and Managerial Accounting

Accounting is broadly classified into **financial accounting** and **managerial (or management) accounting**.

Financial accounting provides financial information to stakeholders outside the company (investors, customers, suppliers, regulators, tax offices, etc.), reporting the situation of management and business. The results of business transactions are

第 1 節　会計とは何か

● 会計は共通言語

　会計は企業の事業活動を包括的に数値で表わす仕組みです。会計により事業活動は数値情報として記録され，企業の内外の人は会計情報を見ることにより事業の活動状況やその業績を把握することができます。そのため会計は事業を行う際に必須の仕組みであり，ビジネスを理解し説明する際に必須のツールです。会計は世界中のビジネスパーソンの共通言語といえます。

● 会計が表わすもの

　会計はさまざまな事業活動の金銭的な価値を数値として示すため，金銭的価値に影響を与えない，または金銭的な価値が把握的できないイベントや取引の結果は会計ではとらえることができません。その意味では，会計は事業活動のすべてを網羅して示すわけではありません。

　会計は地図のようなものといえます。地図は現実にあるすべてのものを示しません。道路標識や街路樹，街並みを含む景色のすべてが地図上に明らかになることはないからです。しかし，地図なしで目的地に到達することは難しいことも確かです。会計は事業のすべてを表わすわけではありませんが，かといって会計を知らずにビジネスを行うことはできないのです。

● 財務会計と管理会計

　会計には大きく**財務会計**（あるいは制度会計）と**管理会計**に分類されます。

　財務会計は，企業外部（投資家，顧客，サプライヤー，規制当局，税務署等）の利害関係者に対して財務情報を提供し経営・事業の状況を報告するためのものです。事業活動における取引の結果は貸借対照表，損益計算書，キャッシュ

summarized in financial statements in a certain format, such as balance sheets, income statements, and cash flow statements. Financial statements are created based on accounting standards and audited by external audit firms. The accounting standard enables various stakeholders to use accounting information with security.

On the other hand, managerial accounting contains information for making management decisions and contemplating necessary measures within the company. Unlike financial accounting, managerial accounting has no standards because the figures are assembled and constructed by various departments according to their necessity and purpose.

This book will discuss financial accounting.

Figure 1.1 | **Financial Accounting and Managerial Accounting**

Financial Accounting	Managerial Accounting
● Reporting on the status of management and business for outsiders ● According to certain standards and formats	● Supporting management decision making and contemplating necessary measures within the company ● Adjusted and devised as needed

○ Reporting Accounting Figures

Typically, a company sets an interval of 1 year as the reporting period of financial performance. The ending date of the fiscal year varies by companies, but about 90% of Japanese companies assign the end of March as the end of the fiscal year to align themselves with the government.

Companies running their business through separate entities in the form of subsidiaries need to report not only the parent company but also the financial performance of subsidiaries and affiliated companies. This type of financial information is known as **consolidated financial statements**. Furthermore, financial statements are generally reported using the currency of the company's home country.

Note that the numbers on financial statements are often truncated, so there may be

フロー計算書という一定の形式に則った財務諸表に取りまとめられます。財務諸表は会計基準に基づいて作成され，外部の監査法人等によって監査されます。このような画一的な会計基準があることにより，さまざまな利害関係者が安心して会計情報を活用することができるのです。

もう一方の管理会計は，企業内部において経営上の意思決定を行ったり，必要な施策を検討・実行したりするための情報を提供するためのものです。管理会計の数値は社内の関係する部署がそれぞれの必要性や目的に応じて組み立てられるものなので，財務会計のような画一的な基準はありません。

本書は財務会計に関して議論していきます。

図表 1.1 ┃ 財務会計と管理会計

財務会計	管理会計
● 企業外部に向けて経営状況，事業状況を報告することが目的	● 企業内部で経営上の意思決定，施策の検討・実行をサポートすることが目的
● 一定の基準と形式に準じており画一的	● 必要に応じて調整され工夫される

◉ 会計数値の報告

通常企業は1年間を財務業績の報告期間（会計年度）として定めています。企業によって会計年度の終了日は異なりますが，日本企業の約9割は政府の会計年度と同じ3月末を年度末としています。

多くの会社は子会社という形で本体とは異なる会社を通じて事業を展開していますが，そのような企業は本体である親会社だけではなく，子会社，関係会社の財務業績もまとめて報告する必要があります。このような財務情報は**連結財務諸表**と呼ばれます。また，財務諸表は一般的に母国の通貨を使用して報告されます。

なお，財務諸表上の数値は切り捨てされることが多いため，合計値や小計値

some differences in the total and subtotal. In addition, negative values are often written with a triangular mark "△" or "▲" in Japanese financial data, while commonly displayed in parentheses in English format. For example, negative 100 is expressed as "△ (or ▲) 100" in Japanese financial statements and "(100)" in English financial statements.

◯ Three Financial Statements

In financial accounting, corporate accounting information is compiled into three main financial statements.

The Balance Sheet (BS) represents a company's assets, liabilities, and shareholders' equity at a particular time. In contrast, **the Income Statement (IS) or Profit and Loss Statement (PL)** shows sales, expenses, and profits over a period of time, while **the Cash Flow Statement (CFS)** represents cash movements over a period of time.

The following sections discuss the contents of these financial statements in detail.

に若干の誤差が生じることがあります。また，日本語の財務諸表においては負の値（マイナスの値）を三角印「△」または「▲」をつけて表記することが多く，一方で，英語表記ではマイナスの表記を括弧で表わすことが一般的です。たとえばマイナス100は，日本語の財務諸表では「△（または▲）100」と表わされ，英語の財務諸表では「(100)」と表わされます。

○ 財務三表

財務会計においては，企業の会計情報は3つの主要な財務諸表に取りまとめられます。

貸借対照表（Balance Sheet, BS）は，「一時点」における企業の資産，負債，資本を表わすものです。それに対して，損益計算書（Income Statement, IS, Profit and Loss Statement, PL）は，「一定期間」における売上高，費用，利益を示し，キャッシュフロー計算書（Cash Flow Statement, CFS）は，「一定期間」における現金の動きを表わします。

以下のセクションではこれらの財務三表の中身を詳細に議論していきます。

2 Balance Sheet

● Balance Sheet Overview

The Balance Sheet (BS) represents a company's financial situation at a particular point in time. Therefore, it is also called **the Statement of Financial Position**. As shown in Figure 1.2, the BS is divided into sections "**Assets**"(left side) and "**Liabilities and Shareholders' Equity** (also referred to as **Net Worth**)" (right side), and the right side is further subdivided into "Liabilities" and "Shareholders' Equity". The amount raised by the company from creditors and shareholders is recorded on the right side of the BS, and the portion attributed to creditors, including banks and suppliers, is classified as a liability. The remaining portion attributed to shareholders is classified under shareholders' equity. The profits made and retained by the company are also recorded under shareholders' equity.

Figure 1.2 | Balance Sheet Overview

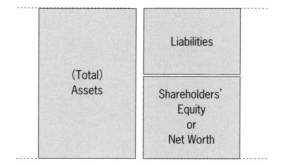

Funds are raised to purchase assets to conduct business activities, which is recorded on the left side of the BS describing how many assets are owned and how they are owned. Assets include current assets such as accounts receivables and inventories, tangible fixed assets such as land and equipment, intangible fixed assets, and long-term financial investments. In addition to assets that occur in a day-to-day operation, assets that can be converted to cash within 1 year are classified as current

第2節 貸借対照表

○ 貸借対照表の概要

　貸借対照表（BS）は，ある一時点における企業の財政状態を表わします。そのため**財政状態計算書**とも呼ばれます。貸借対照表は図表1.2のように「**資産**」（左側）と「**負債及び株主資本（純資産とも呼ばれる）**」（右側）のセクションに分かれており，右側はさらに負債と株主資本に細分化されています。企業が債権者と株主から調達した金額は貸借対照表の右側に記録されます。銀行や仕入先を含む債権者に帰属する分は負債と分類され，その他の残りである株主に帰属する部分は株主資本に分類されます。企業が上げた利益が内部留保されたものも株主資本となります。

図表 1.2 ┃ 貸借対照表の概要

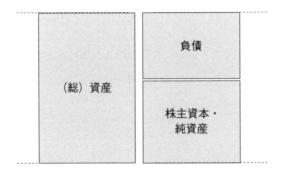

　調達した資金は事業活動を行うための資産購入にあてられますが，どれだけの資産をどのように所有しているのかが貸借対照表の左側に記録されます。企業の資産には売上債権や在庫（棚卸資産）に代表される流動資産や，土地・設備などの有形固定資産，無形固定資産や長期の金融投資が含まれます。日々の営業活動に伴って発生する資産は流動資産に分類されますが，それに加えて現金による精算が行われるまで期間が1年以内の資産は流動資産，それ以外は固

assets, while other assets are classified as fixed assets.

The sum of all assets is always equal to the sum of liabilities and equity. In other words,

$$Assets = Liabilities + Shareholders' \ Equity$$

By definition, this equation always holds, the total assets and the sum of liabilities and shareholders' equity must be "in balance". In order to increase assets, it is necessary to increase liabilities or shareholders' equity (including profits).

● Assets

The left side of the BS represents the assets owned by the company. These assets such as cash, inventory, machinery and equipment, buildings, etc., as well as intangible assets such as software and "rights" with monetary value are recorded here. These assets must be monetarily quantified in value.

In many countries including the U.S. and Japan, assets are listed in the order of the amount of time it would take to convert them into cash (the order of liquidity) as shown in Figure 1.3.

Figure 1.3 | Assets

	Cash
+	Marketable Securities
+	Accounts Receivable
+	Inventories
+	Prepaid Expenses
+	Other Current Assets
=	Current Assets
+	Property, Plant & Equipment
+	Financial Investment
+	Other Fixed Assets
=	Total Assets

定資産に分類されます。

　全資産の合計は常に負債と株主資本の合計と等しくなります。つまり，

$$資産＝負債＋株主資本$$

　定義上，この式は常に成立し，資産と負債と株主資本の合計は「バランス」していなければなりません。資産を増やすためには，負債を増やすか（利益を含めた）株主資本を増やす必要があるということです。

● 資　産

　貸借対照表の左側は，企業が所有している資産を表わします。現金，在庫，機械・設備，建物等といったものに加えて，ソフトウエアのような無形資産，および金銭的価値を持つ，「権利」も含まれます。なお，これらの資産はその価値が金銭的に定量化されていなければなりません。

　米国,日本を含む多くの国では,図表1.3のように資産は現金化されやすい（これを流動性が高いといいます）順番に上から示されます。

図表 1.3 ┃ 資産

```
      現金
  ＋  金融資産（有価証券）
  ＋  売上債権（売掛金）
  ＋  棚卸資産（在庫）
  ＋  前払費用
  ＋  その他流動資産
  ─────────────────
  ＝  流動資産
  ═════════════════
  ＋  有形固定資産
  ＋  金融投資
  ＋  その他固定資産
  ─────────────────
  ＝  資産合計
```

Current assets are assets that occur in an operating activity or those that are converted into cash within 1 year.

Cash is the ultimate liquid asset and includes bank deposits and small cash stored in a drawer.

Marketable securities are liquid financial assets that are expected to be converted to cash within 1 year containing common stocks, bonds and other financial instruments. Financial assets traded in the market, such as stocks and bonds, are called securities. Stocks of an affiliated company and bonds with a maturity period of 1 year or more are classified as **financial investment** in fixed assets.

Most transactions between companies are based on the company's credit, which are transactions paid at a later date. **Accounts receivable** are the accounts of customers who were provided goods or services but have not yet paid for them. When a company ships a product to a customer on credit, the company has the right to collect payment from the customer at a specified time in the future. This right to collect money is reported as accounts receivable.

Inventories include products ready to be sold to customers and the materials in storage to make the products. They are classified into: **raw materials** which are unprocessed materials that will be used in manufacturing products, **work-in-process** which are partially finished products in the process of manufacturing, and **finished goods** which are completed products ready to be shipped to customers.

Prepaid expenses are the amount the company has paid for services that have not yet been received. This includes advance payments for insurance premiums and rent. The right to receive a service going forward is considered as an asset.

Property, plant, and equipment or **PP&E** are things used repeatedly to manufacture, store, and transport products, which includes land, buildings, machinery, equipment, and automobiles. PP&E are evaluated and reported as the purchased price less accumulated depreciation. Accumulated depreciation is the total amount of depreciation since the asset was purchased. Depreciation is an accounting process that distributes acquisition costs across the effective working life of an asset, indicating wear and tear from use which decreases the fixed asset's value over time.

流動資産は，営業活動の中で発生する資産，または1年以内に現金に変換される資産です。

　現金は，究極の流動資産であり，銀行預金や会社の金庫に保管されている小口現金などが含まれます。

　有価証券は，1年以内に現金化されることが想定される流動的な金融商品であり，普通株式，債券やその他の金融商品などが含まれます。なお，株式，債券など市場で取引できる金融資産のことを証券と呼びます。満期日までの期間が1年以上の債券や関連会社株式は固定資産の**金融投資（投資有価証券）**に分類されます。

　企業間の取引は企業の信用に基づいて，代金の支払いは後日となる「掛け」での取引がほとんどです。**売掛金**といった**売上債権**は，製品を出荷あるいはサービスを提供したものの，まだ支払いを受けていない状態の金額です。企業が「掛け売り」で顧客に製品を出荷すると，将来の決められた時点でその顧客から代金を受け取る権利を持ちます。この代金回収の権利が売上債権として示されます。

　棚卸資産（在庫）は，顧客に販売される状態になっている製品や，製品を作るための材料などが含まれます。製品に使用される未加工の材料である**原材料**，製造過程で生じる半製品である**仕掛品**，顧客に出荷できる状態となっている**完成品**といった分類をすることができます。

　前払費用は，まだ受け取っていないサービスに対して会社がすでに支払った金額のことです。保険料支払い，家賃支払いなどの前払い分が該当します。今後サービスを受ける権利を持っているので資産の一部と考えます。

　有形固定資産は，製品の製造，保管，輸送などにおいて繰り返し使用される資産であり，土地，建物，機械，機器，自動車などを含みます。有形固定資産は，取得価格から，減価償却累計額を引いた値で評価および報告されます。減価償却累計額は，資産が購入されてからの減価償却の合計額です。なお，減価償却とは，使用による消耗や時間の経過に伴う固定資産価値の低下を示すものであり，資産の有効な稼働期間全体にわたって取得コストを分散する会計上のプロセスです。この点は第2章で再度説明します。

This will be discussed again in Chapter 2.

Other fixed assets include intangible assets such as computer software, patents, copyrights, and licenses.

Note that even if they were the same asset, the items on the BS are not always the same. The category of accounting items varies depending on the nature and the company's intended use of the asset. For example, the factory land owned by a manufacturing company is categorized as a fixed asset, but it is an inventory for a company that buys and sells real estate. Cars are inventories for car dealers, but fixed assets for car rental companies. Personal computers (PCs) are inventories for PC manufacturers, but PCs used by retailers for cash registers at stores are fixed assets.

The sum of all assets is known as **total assets**.

● Liabilities

The right side of BS consists of liabilities and shareholders' equity.

Figure 1.4 | Liabilities and Shareholders' Equity

	Accounts Payable
+	Accrued Expenses
+	Income Taxes Payable
+	Advanced Payment
+	Current Portion of Debt
+	Other Current Liabilities
= a	Current Liabilities
	Long-term Debt
+	Other Fixed Liabilities
= b	Fixed Liabilities
a + b = c	Total Liabilities
	Capital Stock
+	Retained Earnings
= d	Shareholders' Equity
c + d	Total Liabilities & Equity

その他固定資産には，コンピュータソフトウエア，特許，著作権，ライセンスなどの無形資産が含まれます。

　なお，同一の資産であったとしても，貸借対照表の項目は常に同じとは限りません。企業にとってその資産がどのような意味をもつのか，資産の性質によって会計項目の区分は異なります。たとえば，製造業が保有する工場用の土地は固定資産ですが，不動産を売買する企業にとっては棚卸資産になります。自動車ディーラーにとって自動車は当然在庫ですが，レンタカー会社にとっては固定資産です。パソコンメーカーにとってパソコンは棚卸資産であり，小売業が店舗でレジに使うパソコンは固定資産です。

　すべての資産の合計は**総資産**とも呼ばれます。

◎　負　債

貸借対照表の右側は，負債と株主資本によって構成されます。

図表1.4 ┃ 負債と株主資本

	仕入債務（買掛金）
＋	未払費用
＋	未払法人所得税
＋	前受金
＋	短期社債・借入金
＋	その他流動負債
＝ a	流動負債
	長期社債・借入金
＋	その他固定負債
＝ b	固定負債
a ＋ b ＝ c	負債合計
	資本金
＋	利益剰余金
＝ d	株主資本合計
c ＋ d	負債及び資本合計

Liabilities represent financial obligations or liabilities that a company has to suppliers, employees, governments, customers, creditors, etc. **Current liabilities** are liabilities that must be paid within one year. Liabilities that are not otherwise "current" are called **fixed liabilities**.

Current liabilities are classified according to whom the company is financially liable. Accounts payable owed to suppliers, accrued expenses owed to employees and others for services, taxes owed to the government, advance payments owed to customers, and short-term corporate bonds and short-term debts owed to lenders are included in current liabilities.

Accounts payable are the opposite of accounts receivable. They are the bills owed to other companies for materials and equipment purchased on credit, but have not yet been paid. Because the company is obligated to pay the supplier at a specified time in the future, it is considered as a liability (again, most transactions between companies are done on credit).

Accrued expenses are financial obligations to employees, accountants, lawyers, etc., and represent future payments in exchange for their services provided, such as salaries.

Income tax payable is the corporate income tax that is a financial obligation to the government that must be paid in the future.

Advanced payment (or unearned revenue) represents money received from the customer in advance of shipping goods or providing services. It is considered as a liability because the company has already received money and is now obligated to provide corresponding products and services.

Financial liabilities, such as corporate bonds and borrowings, also known as **debt**, emerges when a company raises funds by borrowing money from banks or other lenders (creditors). Debt that must be repaid within one year is listed as **current portion of debt** under current liabilities and are otherwise part of fixed liabilities. It should be noted that corporate bonds are issued by companies to borrow money, stipulating the repayment date (named maturity), interest (named coupon) rate, and the date of interest payment, at the time of issuance. Different from bank borrowing,

負債は，企業が仕入先，従業員，政府，顧客，債権者などに対して負っている金銭的な義務，債務を表わします。**流動負債**は，1年以内に支払わなければならない債務です。それ以外の「流動」ではない負債は**固定負債**と呼ばれます。

　流動負債は，企業が誰に対して金銭的責任を負っているのかに応じて分類されます。仕入先に対する債務である仕入債務，従業員およびその他のサービスに対する債務である未払費用，政府に対する債務である未払法人所得税，顧客に対する債務である前受金，そして，貸し手，債権者に対する債務である短期の社債や短期の借入金が含まれます。

　買掛金とも呼ばれる**仕入債務**は，売上債権の逆であり，仕入先から材料などを購入したものの，まだ支払いを行っていない状態の金額です。企業は将来の決められた時点において仕入先に代金を支払う義務を負っているので債務です（繰り返しますが，企業間のほとんどの取引は「掛け」によって行われます）。

　未払費用は，従業員や会計士，弁護士などに対する金銭的義務であり，給与や支払いなど，提供されたサービスの対価として今後発生する支払い額を表わします。

　未払法人所得税は，今後支払う予定である法人所得税などであり，政府に対する金銭的義務です。

　前受金（あるいは前受収益）は，製品の出荷またはサービスの提供の前に顧客から受け取った金額を表わします。すでに金額は受け取ってしまっており，それに対応する製品・サービスを提供する義務を負っているため債務の一種と考えます。

　社債・借入金といった金融負債は，銀行や債権者から資金を借りることによって会社が資金を調達する際に生じる負債です。1年以内に返済する必要がある金融負債は**短期社債・借入金**として流動負債に分類され，それ以外は固定負債の一部となります。なお，社債は，企業が資金を借りるために発行する債券であり，発行時に返済日（償還日ともいう），利子率，利息（クーポンという）の支払い日が決まっています。銀行借入と異なって債権者が分散されることが多いですが，企業にとって実質的に借金といえます。

creditors are often dispersed, but it is essentially the same as borrowing.

Small and relatively insignificant liabilities are combined and collectively shown as **other (current or fixed) liabilities**.

○ Shareholders' Equity

Shareholders' equity represents the value of a company belonging to the shareholders who are the owners of the company, however, unlike liabilities, the company is not obligated to repay. Shareholders' equity may also be expressed as **net worth** or simply **equity**, depending on the accounting standards in which they are governed. It consists mainly of capital stock which is funded by shareholders, and retained earnings which is the cumulative amount of profits generated by the company.

Capital stock is the original amount that the owner or shareholder of the company contributed as an investment in the stock (or share) of the company. Any investor who purchases the company's shares becomes a shareholder of the company and has voting rights on important corporate decisions.

Retained earnings are the cumulative amount of all profits previously generated and retained by the company. A company distributes a portion of the profits it generates to shareholders as dividends. Profits retained in the company without being distributed to shareholders will be incorporated into the shareholders' equity. If a company suffers from loss, the value of shareholders' equity will be damaged and the amount will decrease. A company can pay dividends only if it has sufficient retained earnings in the BS.

Shareholders' equity is expressed by:

Shareholders' Equity = Capital Stock + Profit Earned − Dividends

In other words, shareholders' equity increases by issuing (selling) new shares to investors or making a profit. On the other hand, shareholders' equity decreases by recording a loss or paying dividends to shareholders.

比較的小額なその他の負債は，その他（流動または固定）負債としてまとめて示されます。

● 株主資本

　株主資本は，企業の所有者である株主に属する会社の価値を表わし，負債とは異なり，企業は株主に返済する義務がありません。株主資本は準拠する会計基準によって，純資産や単に資本と表記されることもあります。主に株主からの出資金である資本金と，企業が生み出した利益の累積額である利益剰余金によって構成されます。

　資本金は，企業の所有者である株主が会社の株式への投資として拠出した元々の金額です。会社の株式を購入した投資家は，その会社の株主となり，企業の重要な意思決定の際に議決権を持ちます。

　利益剰余金は，これまでに企業が生み出してかつ会社に留保されたすべての利益の累積額です。企業は生み出した利益の一部を配当として株主に分配します。株主に分配されずに企業に留め置かれた利益は株主資本の一部に組み込まれるということです。もし企業が利益を上げられず，損失を計上する場合には，株主資本の価値は毀損され，その額は減少していきます。なお，十分な利益剰余金が貸借対照表上にない場合は，企業は配当を支払うことができません。

　株主資本は以下のように表わされます。

株主資本＝資本金＋稼ぎ出された利益額－配当

　つまり，株主資本は，投資家に対して新たな株式を発行する（売り出す）か，利益を上げることにより増加します。一方で，損失を計上したり，株主に配当金を支払ったりすると株主資本は減少します。

A company may also buy back its shares once they have been sold. This is called share buyback or repurchase and has the same effect of reducing shareholders' equity as dividend payments. This concept will be revisited in Chapter 2.

○ Book Value and Market Value

The balance sheet represents the **book value** or recorded value of an acquired asset, which is usually different from the **market value** at which it is currently valued. Note that the market value of a company is determined by the cash flow it is expected to generate in the future but the figure that is recorded on the BS is based on the historical purchase price or the original value of the asset.

また，第2章で紹介しますが，企業は一度売り出した自社の株式を買い戻すこともあります。これは自己株式の取得または自社株買いと呼ばれ，配当の支払いと同様に株主資本を減少させる効果があります。

● 簿価と時価

　貸借対照表は，取得した資産の帳簿上の価値を表わすものであり，その価値は通常その時点の価値である**時価**とは異なります。企業の価値は将来生み出されると期待されるキャッシュフローによって決まるのですが，そうした時価とは異なり，貸借対照表にはその資産を取得した価格，もともとの価格が記録されます。なお，取得した資産の帳簿上の価値のことを**簿価**と呼びます。

Income Statement

Income Statement Overview

The Income Statement (IS) or Profit and Loss Statement (PL) shows sales, expenses, and profits (also called income or earnings) of a company over a period of time (year, quarter, month, etc.) and reveals whether a company has made a profit or a loss.

The IS calculates the profit by deducting the expenses from the sales revenue during that period. In other words,

$$Sales - Expenses = Profit$$

As shown in Figure 1.5, income from operations is calculated by subtracting the cost of goods sold, which is an expense directly related to sales, and selling, general, and administrative expenses associated with operating activities during that period from sales. Net income is calculated by adding non-operating profit such as receiving interest, deducting non-operating expenses such as interest payments to operating income, and deducting taxes, while taking into account non-recurring items.

Figure 1.5 | Income Statements

	Sales (Revenue)
-	Cost of Goods Sold
=	Gross Margin
-	Selling, General & Administrative Expenses
=	Income from Operations
+ / -	Non-operating Profit/Expenses
-	Income Taxes
=	Net Income

第3節 損益計算書

損益計算書の概要

損益計算書（PL）は一定期間（年，四半期，月など）にわたる売上高，費用，利益を示し，企業が利益を生んだのか，損失を出したのかを明らかにするものです。

損益計算書はその期間に販売された額（売上）から，費用を差し引いて利益を算出します。つまり，

$$売上高-費用=利益$$

です。

図表 1.5 に示す通り，売上高から売上に直接的に関係する費用である売上原価とその期間における販売費・一般管理費（販管費）といった営業活動に伴う費用を差し引いたものが営業利益です。営業利益に利息の受け取りといった営業外利益を加え，利息の支払いといった営業外費用を差し引き，一時的に発生する非経常的な項目があれば加味し，税金を差し引くと当期純利益が計算されます。

図表 1.5 ┃ 損益計算書

```
    売上高（営業収益）
 －  売上原価
─────────────────────
 ＝  売上総利益
 －  販管費
─────────────────────
 ＝  営業利益
＋／－ 営業外損益
 －  法人所得税等
─────────────────────
 ＝  当期純利益
```

● Sales

Any company delivers some kind of product or service as its core business, and this volume of delivery known as **sale** is also referred to as **sales revenue** or simply **revenue**.

Sales are expressed in the IS when a company delivers products or provides services to customers. Orders received from customers do not change the IS. Sales are accounted for when the ordered product is actually shipped or provided.

Providing a product or service entitles you to receive payment from the customer unless you receive cash immediately. This is recorded in the BS as accounts receivable (on the other hand, the customer records the same amount as accounts payable since it is obligated to pay the price in the future).

● Expenses

Costs of goods sold (COGS) or **cost of sales** is what you spend when you buy or make products. This includes expenditures for raw materials, factory workers' wages, and manufacturing overheads. The cost to purchase and manufacture products accumulates as inventories until the product is sold. When this inventory is sold (provided) to the customer, the cost is taken out of inventory and entered in the IS as a cost. Because these types of expenses are spent to earn revenue, costs are only recognized when the sales occur, which is called the matching principle in accounting.

Gross margin or **gross profit** is the amount left over from sales after COGS are subtracted, indicating the company's ability to add value to the costs that are directly associated with sales.

Selling, general, and administrative (SG&A) expenses otherwise known as **operating expenses**, are expenditures that a company makes to generate income but does not directly associate with individual sales transactions (shipments). SG&A

● 売上高

　どんな企業であれ，コアビジネスとして何らかの製品・サービスを販売しており，この額が**売上高**です。売上高は**営業収益**とも呼ばれます。

　売上高は，企業が顧客に製品を出荷したり，サービスを提供したりすると損益計算書に表われます。顧客から注文を受ける受注だけでは，損益計算書は変化しません。注文した製品を実際に出荷したり，サービスを提供したりした時点で売上高は計上されます。

　製品・サービスを提供すると，その時点で対価としての現金を受け取らない限り，顧客から代金を受け取る権利が発生します。これは売上債権として貸借対照表に計上されます（製品・サービスの提供を受けた顧客企業にとっては代金の支払い義務が発生するため，この額は仕入債務となります）。

● 費　用

　売上原価は，商品の購入費や製品を製造する際に費やした金額です。ここには原材料，工場労働者の賃金，製造間接費などの支出が含まれます。商品の購入費や製品を製造するためのコストは，製品が販売されるまで棚卸資産として蓄積され，この在庫が顧客に販売（提供）されると，そのコストは在庫から取り出され，原価として損益計算書に入力されます。これらのコストは収益を得るために費やされているので，売上が発生したタイミングで原価を認識するのです。この考え方は，会計における費用収益対応の原則と呼ばれます。

　売上高から売上原価を差し引いた金額は**売上総利益**あるいは**粗利**または**粗利益**と呼ばれます。粗利益は，売上に直接関連するコストに対して会社がどれだけの価値を付加したのかを示します。

　販売費・一般管理費（販管費）は**営業費用**とも呼ばれ，企業が売上を生み出すことに関係はするものの，個別の販売取引（出荷）に直接的に対応しない支出です。販管費は期間に対応するコスト（期間費用）であり，棚卸資産として

expenses correspond to the period (period costs), and are recorded directly in the IS during the period in which the expense occurred (not as inventories).

SG&A expenses are generally grouped into sales & marketing, research & development (R&D), and general and administrative expenses. Sales & marketing expenses include sales persons' salaries, sales commission, and advertising fees. R&D expenses include researchers' salaries and the purchase of materials for R&D. General and administrative expenses include staff salaries and operating expenses in the Human Resources, General Affairs, and Accounting departments, etc.

○ Incomes

Income from operations or operating income refers to what is left over after COGS and SG&A expenses are subtracted from sales. It is the profits a company generates from its core business functions. If the sales exceed the expenses, the business is profitable. Meanwhile, if the expenses exceed the sales, a loss has occurred.

Sales are earned by a company's core business, however, a company may also generate income and have expenses from non-operating activities. For example, paying interest on debt is outside the scope of regular day-to-day operations (activities related to corporate financing are called financial activities as described in the next section, cash flow statement). Therefore, paying interest on a loan is a **non-operating expense**, while receiving interest on bank deposits owned by the company is a **non-operating profit (income)**.

Net income is the profit after deducting corporate **income taxes**. Corporate income tax is calculated by multiplying pretax profits by the corporate tax rate, which varies by country. Net income represents the final result of IS (accounting bottom line).

Figure 1.6 summarize various profits.

計上されるのではなく，費用が発生した期間に直接損益計算書に計上されます。

　販管費は一般的に販売費・広告宣伝費，研究開発費，一般管理費に分類されます。販売費・広告宣伝費には，営業人員の給与や販売手数料，広告料などが含まれます。研究開発費は，研究者の給与，研究開発用材料の購入などからなります。一般管理費には，人事・総務・会計部署のスタッフの給与や運営コストなどが含まれます。

● 利　益

　売上高から売上原価と販管費を差し引いたものが**営業利益**です。本業から得られる利益といえ，売上が費用を超えている場合に事業は利益を得ることができ，費用が売上を上回った場合にはその事業は損失を生み出していることになります。

　売上高は，企業が行っている事業において生み出された収入ですが，企業は，財務活動や通常の営業活動以外からも収益を生み出すことも，支出を行うこともあります。たとえば，金融負債に対する利息の支払いは，営業上の基本的な日常業務の範囲外といえます（次節の「キャッシュフロー計算書」で説明しますが企業の資金調達にかかわる活動は財務活動と呼ばれます）。そのため，借入金に対する利息の支払いは**営業外費用**となり，反対に会社が所有する銀行預金に対する利息の受け取りは**営業外利益**となります。

　さらに**法人所得税**などの税金を差し引いたものが**当期純利益**です。法人所得税は税引き前の利益に，国によって異なる法人税率を掛け合わせて計算されます。当期純利益は，損益計算書の最終結果（会計上の最終的な利益）を表わします。

　図表1.6はさまざまな利益をまとめて表わしています。

Figure 1.6 | Various Profits

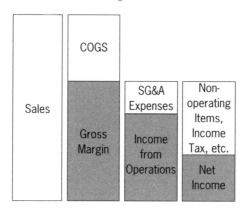

Income Statement and Balance Sheet

As mentioned above, the balance sheet shows the financial situation at a particular point in time, whereas the income statement shows performance over a period of time. So, there is a balance sheet at the beginning and the end of each period. When a company makes a profit, the assets owned by the company increase, and the left side of the BS increases. Since the profit on the IS increases the retained earnings (shareholders' equity), the right side of the BS increases at the same time so that both sides remain in balance.

The IS connects the BS at the beginning and the end of the period.

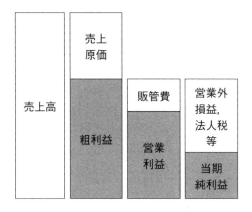

図表 1.6 ┃ さまざまな利益

損益計算書と貸借対照表

前述した通り，貸借対照表は，特定の時点での財政状況を示しているのに対して，損益計算書は一定の期間の業績を示します。一定の期間の初めには期初（あるいは期首）の貸借対照表があり，期間の終わりには期末の貸借対照表があります。企業が利益を上げると，会社が所有する資産が増加し，すなわち貸借対照表の左側が増加します。そして，損益計算書の利益は貸借対照表の右側の利益剰余金（株主資本）を同時に増加させるため，やはり貸借対照表の両側は必ず一致します。

期首と期末の貸借対照表は損益計算書によって接続されているのです。

Cash Flow Statement

● Profit and Cash

Making a profit and increasing cash are not the same. Even a profitable company with lots of net income can go bankrupt (which is called a black-ink bankruptcy). Sales and expenses that make up the accounting profit are measured when an economic event such as a transaction occurs, regardless of the actual movement of cash. This is one of the accounting principles called the accrual principle, or the accrual basis of accounting (on the other hand, the cash principle recognizes revenue and expenses at the time of cash delivery).

● Cash Flow Statement Overview

The Cash Flow Statement (CFS) tracks the movement of cash through the business over a period of time (year, quarter, month…) and indicates whether a company has increased or decreased in cash.

When the cash flow for a period is positive the company's cash at the end of the period is greater at the beginning of the period, and when the cash flow is negative then the opposite is true. If a company's cash flow is continuously negative, it faces a shortage of cash and the risk of bankruptcy increases.

The flow of cash is classified into three categories by its nature: **cash flow from operating activities**, **cash flow from investing activities**, and **cash flow from financing activities**.

In the CFS, if cash enters the company, it will be written as a positive, and if the cash goes out, it will be filled in as a negative. For example, purchasing machinery and paying dividends will be recorded as a negative, while selling assets and borrowings will be positive.

第4節 キャッシュフロー計算書

● 利益と現金

　利益を上げることと現金を増やすことは同じではありません。収益性が高く多くの利益を計上している会社であっても，倒産する可能性があります（黒字倒産と呼ばれます）。会計上の利益を構成する売上，費用は，現金の実際の移動とは関係なく，取引のような経済的事象が発生したときに計上されるからです。これは「発生主義」と呼ばれる会計原則の1つです（これに対するのが収益と費用を現金の受け渡しの時点で認識する「現金主義」です）。

● キャッシュフロー計算書の概要

　キャッシュフロー計算書（CFS）は，一定期間（年，四半期，月）などにわたるビジネスを通じた現金の動きを記録し，企業が現金を増やしたのか減らしたのか，その増減額を示します。

　ある期間のキャッシュフローがプラスの場合，会社は期間の終了時（期末）において期間の開始時（期首）よりも多くの現金を持っているということであり，キャッシュフローがマイナスの場合，期末の現金は期首よりも少なくなっているということです。企業のキャッシュフローが継続的にマイナスの場合，現金が不足し，企業は倒産する危険性が高まります。

　現金の流れはその性質により，**営業活動によるキャッシュフロー**，**投資活動によるキャッシュフロー**，**財務活動によるキャッシュフロー**の3つに分類されて示されます。

　なお，キャッシュフロー計算書上では，企業に現金が入ってくる場合はプラスで，キャッシュが出ていく場合にはマイナスで記入されます。たとえば，機械設備を購入したり配当を支払った時にはマイナス，資産を売却したり追加的な借り入れを行った場合にはプラスとなります。

Figure 1.7 | Cash Flow Statement

	Cash Receipts from Customers
−	Cash Paid to Suppliers and Employees
−	Income Taxes Paid
= A	Cash Flows from Operating Activities
−	Purchase of Property, Plant & Equipment
−	Purchase of Marketable Securities
= B	Cash Flows from Investing Activities
	Increase in Debt
−	Interests Paid
−	Dividends Paid
+	Issuance of Common Stock
= C	Cash Flows from Financing Activities
A + B + C	Change in Cash

○ Cash Transactions and Non-cash Transactions

Only transactions associated with cash movements affect cash flow. Transactions without cash movements (called non-cash transactions) do not affect cash flow.

Many non-cash transactions affect the IS and the BS, even if they do not change the CFS. For example, when a company ships a product, sales are recorded on the IS, which increases accounts receivables on the BS, but the CFS does not change. It is only when a customer pays for the product that the CFS changes which also causes a decrease in accounts receivables on the BS (however, there is no effect on the IS at that time).

○ Cash Flow from Operating Activities

Cash flow from operating activities (or operating CF or CF from operation) represents the amount of cash generated in daily operating activities. The normal day-to-day activities (manufacturing and sales of products) conducted for a business are called its operations.

図表 1.7 ┃ キャッシュフロー計算書

	売上収入
－	経費の支払いによる支出
－	法人所得税等の支払い
＝ A	営業活動によるキャッシュフロー
－	固定資産の取得
－	金融資産の取得
＝ B	投資活動によるキャッシュフロー
	借入金・社債の増加
－	利息支払い
－	配当支払い
＋	株式の発行
＝ C	財務活動によるキャッシュフロー
A＋B＋C	現金の増減額

● 現金取引と非現金取引

　キャッシュフローに影響するのは現金の動きを伴う取引のみです。現金の動きを伴わない取引（非現金取引）はキャッシュフローに影響を与えません。

　しかし，多くの非現金取引はキャッシュフロー計算書に変化を与えないとしても，損益計算書や貸借対照表には影響を与えます。たとえば，会社が製品を出荷すると損益計算書上で売上高が計上され，貸借対照表上の売上債権が発生しますが，キャッシュフローは変化しません。顧客がその製品の代金を支払うとき売上債権が減少し，キャッシュフローは変化するのです（しかし，この時は損益計算書には何の影響もありません）。

● 営業活動によるキャッシュフロー

　営業活動によるキャッシュフロー（営業 CF）は日々の営業活動を行うことによって生み出される現金の額を表わします。なお，事業にかかわる日常業務（製品の製造や販売）のことを営業活動といいます。

Cash receipts from customers are cash inflows associated with business operations, coming from collecting money from customers. The company's cash balance increases by the number of cash receipts and also decreases accounts receivables recorded on the BS.

Cash paid to suppliers and employees are cash expenditures used for business operations such as payments for materials, equipment, rent, and salaries. The cash balance of the company decreases from this expenditure whereas accounts payables and accrued expenses recorded on the BS decrease.

Income taxes paid represents the amount of tax payment made to the government. Cash does not decrease simply by owing a tax payment and accruing it in the IS. The company's cash only decreases when the taxes are actually paid.

○ Cash Flow from Investing Activities

Cash flow from investing activities (or investing CF) shows how and how much cash invested in assets that are not part of daily operations. A company makes long-term investments to constantly increase its capacity to generate profits and earn cash, which are then aggregated into investing activities.

Purchase of property, plant, and equipment is cash outflow invested in the acquisition of tangible and intangible fixed assets such as manufacturing equipment, machinery, land, buildings, and software.

Cash used for the **purchase of marketable securities** is classified as one item of investing CF.

When cash is utilized to purchase assets, the company's cash balance decreases. Conversely, when fixed assets or securities are sold, the cash balance of the company increases.

○ Cash Flow from Financing Activities

Cash flow from financing activities (or financing CF) represents where a company

売上収入は事業運営による現金収入であり，顧客からの売上代金回収にあたります。売上収入の分だけ会社の現金残高は増加し，貸借対照表上に計上されていた売上債権は減少します。

　経費の支払いによる支出は，事業運営に使用される現金支出であり，材料や備品，家賃，給与などの支払い額にあたります。支出分だけ会社の現金残高は減少し，貸借対照表上に計上されていた仕入債務や未払費用は減少します。

　法人所得税等の支払いは政府に対する税金の支払い額を表わします。損益計算書において会計上支払うべき税金を確定し計上しただけでは現金が減りません。実際に税金を支払うことにより，会社の現金は減少します。

● 投資活動によるキャッシュフロー

　投資活動によるキャッシュフロー（投資 CF）は日常業務の一部とはいえない資産への投資をどれだけどのように行ったのかを示します。企業は利益を上げ，現金を稼ぐための能力を常に高めていなければならず，そのための長期的な投資を行っていく必要があり，それらの活動は投資活動に集約されます。

　固定資産の取得は製造設備，機械，備品，土地・建物やソフトウエアなどの有形・無形固定資産の取得に投じられた金額です。

　有価証券の購入に使用される現金は，**金融資産の取得**として投資 CF の 1 項目に分類されます。

　資産の購入に資金が投じられれば企業の現金残高は減少します。逆に固定資産や有価証券を売却した場合には，企業の現金残高は増加することになります。

● 財務活動によるキャッシュフロー

　財務活動によるキャッシュフロー（財務 CF）は，企業が資金をどこからど

raises their funds from, and how much funds are raised. It also represents the sum and the destination of where this money is repaid. This includes issuing (selling) shares to investors, borrowing money from banks, and paying dividends, etc.

A company borrows money from banks or issues (sells) corporate bonds to investors in capital markets to raise necessary funds. This increases cash in the company and is recorded as an **increase in debt**. On the other hand, when a company repays its debts, the company's cash decreases.

Borrowings and bonds are accompanied by interest payments. When a company pays interest, cash decreases and is recorded as **interests paid**.

When a company distributes a portion of its profits as dividends to shareholders, the company's cash is decreased which is recorded as **dividends paid**.

Funds raised by a company through issuing shares to investors is recorded as an **issuance of common stock**, and the cash balance of the company increases.

● Cash Flow Statement and Balance Sheet

The actual CFS calculates the cash balance at the end of the period by adding cash received during the period to the cash balance at the beginning of the period, and then by deducting the cash paid during the period. In other words,

Beginning Cash Balance + Cash Receipt − Cash Paid = Ending Cash Balance

The beginning and ending balance of cash matches the amount at the beginning and the ending of the BS, respectively.

れだけ調達し，またどこにどれだけ返済・還元を行ったのかを表わします。投資家への株式の発行（売却）や銀行からの資金の借り入れ，配当金の支払いなどが含まれます。

　企業は銀行からお金を借りたり，あるいは資本市場で投資家に対して社債を発行（売却）して資金調達を行います。これらは会社における現金を増加させ，**借入金・社債の増加**として記録されます。反対に企業が借り入れを返済すると，会社の現金は減少します。

　借入金や社債には利息の支払いが伴います。企業が利息を支払えば現金は減少し，**利息支払い**として記録されます。

　企業が利益の一部を株主に配当として分配すると企業の現金は減少し，**配当支払い**として記録されます。

　企業が投資家に株式を発行して調達した資金は，**株式の発行**として記録され，企業の現金残高は増加します。

● キャッシュフロー計算書と貸借対照表

　実際のキャッシュフロー計算書は，期間の開始時（期首）における現金残高に期間中に受け取った現金を加え，期間中に支払った現金を差し引いて期間の終了時（期末）の現金残高を計算します。つまり，

$$期首現金残高＋現金収入－現金支出＝期末現金残高$$

です。

　なお，期首期末の現金残高はいずれもそれぞれの時点における貸借対照表の現金残高と一致します。

Figure 1.8 | Format of Cash Flow Statement

A	Cash Flow from Operating Activities
B	Cash Flow from Investing Activities
C	Cash Flow from Financing Activities
D = A + B + C	Change in Cash
E	Beginning Cash Balance
F = D + E	Ending Cash Balance

● Free Cash Flow (FCF)

Let's touch on **free cash flow (FCF)**, which is frequently used in the area of corporate finance. FCF is focused on by a company when evaluating the value of its investment and assets. FCF is calculated by deducting the capital expenditure required for the business from the operating CF that is generated over a period of time. In other words, FCF is defined as;

$$FCF = \text{Operating CF} - \text{Capital Expenditures}$$

and indicates the cash left over that can be returned to investors from the cash earned. FCF is close to the sum of the operating CF and the investing CF, and a negative FCF means a cash shortage. A company whose FCF is negative needs additional financing to sustain its business.

FCF is a theoretical basis for valuing assets or companies. The current value of future FCF stream determines the value of a company or business (see a finance text for more details).

図表 1.8 ┃ キャッシュフロー計算書の形式

A	営業活動によるキャッシュフロー
B	投資活動によるキャッシュフロー
C	財務活動によるキャッシュフロー
D = A + B + C	現金増減額
E	期首現金残高
F = D + E	期末現金残高

● フリー・キャッシュフロー（FCF）

　ここで，コーポレートファイナンスの分野で頻繁に使用される**フリー・キャッシュフロー（FCF）**について触れておきましょう。FCF は企業が投資や資産の価値を評価する際に注目する数値であり，一期間において生み出された営業 CF から，事業に必要な投資額を差し引いて計算されます。つまり，

$$FCF ＝営業 CF －設備投資額$$

と定義され，稼いだキャッシュの中から投資を行い，その後に残った投資家に還元可能なキャッシュを意味します。FCF は営業 CF と投資 CF の合計額に近い数値であり，FCF がマイナスならば必要な資金が不足していることになります。FCF がマイナスの企業が事業を継続していくためには，追加的な資金調達が必要だということです。

　FCF は資産や企業を価値評価する際の理論的な基盤であり，将来の FCF の現時点における価値が企業や事業の価値を決定します（より詳細にはファイナンスのテキストを参照ください）。

5 Getting Financial Data

Where is Financial Data Available?

Financial information, including a company's financial statements is summarized in official current reports and annual filings, or **annual reports** prepared independently by the company. These reports are usually disclosed on the company's website if it is a publicly listed company whose stock is traded in the stock exchange market.

The report is also aggregated on the websites of government agencies. If it is a U.S. company, visit the Securities and Exchange Commission page "EDGAR", and search by company name.

(https://www.sec.gov/edgar/searchedgar/companysearch.html)

If it is a Japanese company, you can rely on the Financial Service Agency's page "EDINET", where financial statements for all listed companies are available.

(https://disclosure.edinet-fsa.go.jp/)

Yahoo! Finance and Bloomberg also provide accounting information free of charge in a standard format on its their websites. Financial information is readily available as long as it is not detailed information.

Form 10-K

If you try to find financial information, you may be surprised that there are too many types of reports. A company is required to report financial results yearly and quarterly, as well as the shareholders' meeting resolutions, and other important events.

Among the numerous files, Form **10-K** contains comprehensive financial information for the fiscal year, and therefore, is most commonly used for corporate financial performance analysis.

第**5**節 財務情報の入手

● 財務情報はどこにあるのか

　企業の財務三表を含む財務情報は，外部への公式な報告書である決算短信や有価証券報告書，または企業独自に用意される**アニュアルレポート**といった報告書にまとめられています。これらの報告書は，上場企業であれば通常は企業のホームページに開示されています。

　また，報告書は政府機関のホームページにも集約されています。米国企業であれば証券取引委員会のページ「EDGAR」を訪ね，企業名から検索できます。
（https://www.sec.gov/edgar/searchedgar/companysearch.html）

　日本企業であれば金融庁のページ「EDINET」に上場企業すべての財務決算書類がまとめられています。
（https://disclosure.edinet-fsa.go.jp/）

　Yahoo! ファイナンスやブルームバーグといったインターネット上のサイトでも，統一フォーマットで会計情報が無料で提供されていますので，財務情報の概略であれば容易に入手可能です。

● 有価証券報告書

　財務情報を探そうとすると，あまりにも多くの報告書があることに驚くかもしれません。企業は年次での情報に加えて，四半期の決算情報，株主総会での決議の内容，その他の重要なイベントについても報告が求められるからです。

　数多くの報告書類の中にあって，会計年度全体の包括的な情報を含んだ書類は**有価証券報告書**です。これは企業の財務分析の際に最も一般的に使用されます。

Chapter 2

Recording Business Activities

How do transactions change the financial statements?

- In this chapter, we will follow a story of a fictitious company to understand how business activities are recorded in each of the financial statements discussed in the previous chapter.

- Some of these activities affect all three financial statements, while others affect only one of them. Through analysis of these activities, you will see how the three financial statements are mutually related.

- In the following scenario, let's assume that you will start a rice cracker manufacturing company and observe how accounting information is created by the subsequent activities.

第 2 章

事業活動の記録

取引はどのように財務三表に変化を与えるのか

★★

- 本章では，前章で学んだ財務三表に，1つひとつの事業活動の内容がどのように記録されていくのかを，架空の企業の事業ストーリーに沿って確認していきます。

- 活動によっては，財務三表すべてに影響を及ぼすものもあれば，そのうちの1つだけに影響を与えるものもあります。これらの事業活動の記録を通じて，三表が相互に関係していることも確認できます。

- 以下では，皆さんが「せんべい屋」を創業すると仮定し，その後の活動，取引がどのような会計情報になっていくのかを見ていきましょう。

Introduction
Showa Senbei Corporation

You traveled to Niigata Prefecture, an area known for its rice production, and are fascinated by senbei, a traditional Japanese confectionery made from rice and seasoned with soy sauce.

With a strong passion to deliver delicious rice crackers to as many people as possible, you decided to produce your own tasty and healthy rice crackers. In order to accomplish this goal, you prepared funding to establish "Showa Senbei Corporation" which makes and sells senbei.

The next page onward reveals how each business activity of Showa Senbei is recorded on the BS, IS, and CFS.

The top half of the page describes a specific activity and the bottom half demonstrates how each of these three financial statements change in line with the activity. Financial statements show values in three columns: the state before the activity occurred, the change due to the activity, and the state after the activity.

This chapter shows the IS and CFS on the left page and BS on the right page due to a space limitation.

Most activities are followed by an application exercise containing slight modifications from the original activity. Please think about how condition changes create differences when recording the financial statements. These application exercises are independent from the story, therefore, the results of these exercises only indicate the amount of change caused by the activity.

As a starter, let's consider the scene of establishing the company.

　日本の米どころ新潟県に旅行したあなたは，現地で出会った米を原材料として作られる醤油で味付けされた日本の伝統的なお菓子，せんべいに心を奪われました。

　あなたは，多くの人に美味しいせんべいを届けたいと思い，独自の美味しく健康的なせんべいを生産することにしました。そしてその思いを実現するために，現金を集め，せんべいを作って販売する会社，株式会社昭和せんべいを設立しました。

　次ページ以降では，「昭和せんべい」の事業活動に沿って，1つひとつの活動がどのように貸借対照表（BS），損益計算書（PL），キャッシュフロー計算書（CFS）に記録されていくのかを確認していきます。

　ページの上半分で活動に関して説明し，ページの下半分ではどのように財務三表が変化するのかを示します。財務三表では，その活動が起こる前の状態，その活動による変化，その活動の後の状態という3列において数値が示されます。各活動の後の数値は，それに続く活動の前の状態ということになります。

　なお，この章ではスペースの都合上，見開きの左ページに損益計算書とキャッシュフロー計算書を，右ページに貸借対照表を記載しています。

　ほとんどの活動に関しては，応用問題として，活動の条件を若干変化させたケースを用意しています。取引の内容の変化によって財務三表への記録のされ方がどのように変化するのか考えてみてください。なお応用問題は全体のストーリーとは独立しており，そのため活動による変化額のみを示します。

　ではまず手始めに，会社設立の場面を考えてみましょう。

You have completed the legal procedure for establishing a Showa Senbei.

You personally invest $100,000 in cash on hand into the company and purchase 100,000 shares at $1 per share with your investment.

- Your money goes to Showa Senbei, which is a separate legal entity from you, so now Showa Senbei has $100,000 in cash through the issuance of common stock (A in the figure below).
- The cash balance increases (B), and the capital stock of shareholders' equity increases (C) which is recorded on Showa Senbei's BS.

Showa Senbei sells (issues) the shares to you in return for your investment which makes you the founder, the owner (shareholder), and the chief executive officer of the company.

Income Statement	損益計算書	Foundation 設立
Sales (Revenue)	売上高（営業収益）	
− Cost of Goods Sold	売上原価	
= Gross Margin	売上総利益	0
− Selling, General & Administrative Expenses	販管費	
= Income from Operations	営業利益	0
+/− Non-operating Profit/Expenses	営業外損益	
− Income Taxes	法人所得税等	
= Net Income	当期純利益	0

Cash Flow Statement	キャッシュフロー計算書	Foundation 設立
Cash Receipts from Customers	売上収入	
− Cash Paid to Suppliers and Employees	経費の支払いによる支出	
− Income Taxes Paid	法人所得税等の支払い	
=A Cash Flows from Operating Activities	営業活動によるキャッシュフロー	0
− Purchase of Property, Plant & Equipment	固定資産の取得	
− Purchase of Marketable Securities	金融資産の取得	
=B Cash Flows from Investing Activities	投資活動によるキャッシュフロー	0
Increase in Debt	借入金・社債の増加	
− Interests Paid	利息支払い	
− Dividends Paid	配当支払い	
+ Issuance of Common Stock	株式の発行	**A** 100,000
=C Cash Flows from Financing Activities	財務活動によるキャッシュフロー	100,000
A+B+C Change in Cash	現金の増減額	100,000

⓪ 「昭和せんべい」設立

あなたは「昭和せんべい」の会社設立に関する法的手続きを完了しました。

あなたは手持ちの現金100,000ドルを出資します。この100,000ドルを用いて，1株あたり1ドルで100,000株を購入しました。

● あなたの現金はあなたとは別の法人格である「昭和せんべい」に渡り，「昭和せんべい」は株式発行（表中A）により100,000ドルの現金を手に入れます。

● 「昭和せんべい」のBSにおいて現金残高が増加し（B），株主資本のうちの資本金が増加します（C）。

「昭和せんべい」は出資金と引き換えに株式をあなたに売却（発行）し，あなたは「昭和せんべい」の株式を所有します。あなたは創業者であり，会社の所有者（株主）であり，最高経営責任者でもあるということです。

	Balance Sheet	貸借対照表	Foundation 設立
	Cash	現金	B 100,000
+	Marketable Securities	金融資産（有価証券）	
+	Accounts Receivable	売上債権（売掛金）	
+	Inventories	棚卸資産（在庫）	
+	Prepaid Expenses	前払費用	
+	Other Current Assets	その他流動資産	
=	Current Assets	流動資産	100,000
+	Property, Plant & Equipment	有形固定資産	
+	Financial Investment	金融投資	
+	Other Fixed Assets	その他固定資産	
=	Total Assets	資産合計	100,000
	Accounts Payable	仕入債務（買掛金）	
+	Accrued Expenses	未払費用	
+	Income Taxes Payable	未払法人所得税	
+	Advanced Payment	前受金	
+	Current Portion of Debt	短期社債・借入金	
+	Other Current Liabilities	その他流動負債	
=a	Current Liabilities	流動負債	0
	Long-term Debt	長期社債・借入金	
+	Other Fixed Liabilities	その他固定負債	
=b	Fixed Liabilities	固定負債	0
a+b=c	Total Liabilities	負債合計	0
	Capital Stock	資本金	C 100,000
+	Retained Earnings	利益剰余金	
=d	Shareholders' Equity	株主資本合計	100,000
c+d	Total Liabilities & Equity	負債及び資本合計	100,000

Activity 0: Application Exercise

Other investors offer to invest in Showa Senbei. The investors are willing to provide $600,000 to Showa Senbei, in exchange for 200,000 shares (paying $3 per share).

How do the financial statements change?

You already own 100,000 shares. How does accepting this investor's offer change your ownership?

	Income Statement	損益計算書	0 Exercise 0 応用問題
	Sales (Revenue)	売上高（営業収益）	
−	Cost of Goods Sold	売上原価	
=	Gross Margin	売上総利益	0
−	Selling, General & Administrative Expenses	販管費	
=	Income from Operations	営業利益	0
+/−	Non-operating Profit/Expenses	営業外損益	
−	Income Taxes	法人所得税等	
=	Net Income	当期純利益	0

	Cash Flow Statement	キャッシュフロー計算書	0 Exercise 0 応用問題
	Cash Receipts from Customers	売上収入	
−	Cash Paid to Suppliers and Employees	経費の支払いによる支出	
−	Income Taxes Paid	法人所得税等の支払い	
=A	Cash Flows from Operating Activities	営業活動によるキャッシュフロー	0
−	Purchase of Property, Plant & Equipment	固定資産の取得	
−	Purchase of Marketable Securities	金融資産の取得	
=B	Cash Flows from Investing Activities	投資活動によるキャッシュフロー	0
	Increase in Debt	借入金・社債の増加	
−	Interests Paid	利息支払い	
−	Dividends Paid	配当支払い	
+	Issuance of Common Stock	株式の発行	600,000
=C	Cash Flows from Financing Activities	財務活動によるキャッシュフロー	600,000
A+B+C	Change in Cash	現金の増減額	600,000

Showa Senbei has a total of 300,000 shares issued, of which you own 100,000 shares, so you will now own one-third (33.3％) of the company.

別の投資家から「昭和せんべい」に出資したいとの申し出がありました。投資家は「昭和せんべい」の株式 200,000 株と交換に現金 600,000 ドルを提供してくれるそうです（1 株あたり 3 ドルを支払うということです）。

財務三表はどのように変化しますか？

あなたはすでに 100,000 株を所有しています。この投資家の申し出を受け入れると，所有権はどのように変わりますか？

	Balance Sheet	貸借対照表	0 Exercise 0 応用問題
	Cash	現金	600,000
+	Marketable Securities	金融資産（有価証券）	
+	Accounts Receivable	売上債権（売掛金）	
+	Inventories	棚卸資産（在庫）	
+	Prepaid Expenses	前払費用	
+	Other Current Assets	その他流動資産	
=	Current Assets	流動資産	600,000
+	Property, Plant & Equipment	有形固定資産	
+	Financial Investment	金融投資	
+	Other Fixed Assets	その他固定資産	
=	Total Assets	資産合計	600,000
	Accounts Payable	仕入債務（買掛金）	
+	Accrued Expenses	未払費用	
+	Income Taxes Payable	未払法人所得税	
+	Advanced Payment	前受金	
+	Current Portion of Debt	短期社債・借入金	
+	Other Current Liabilities	その他流動負債	
=a	Current Liabilities	流動負債	0
	Long-term Debt	長期社債・借入金	
+	Other Fixed Liabilities	その他固定負債	
=b	Fixed Liabilities	固定負債	0
a+b=c	Total Liabilities	負債合計	0
	Capital Stock	資本金	600,000
+	Retained Earnings	利益剰余金	
=d	Shareholders' Equity	株主資本合計	600,000
c+d	Total Liabilities & Equity	負債及び資本合計	600,000

「昭和せんべい」の発行株式は合計で 300,000 株となり，そのうちあなたは 100,000 株を所有していますので，所有権は 3 分の 1 となります。

Showa Senbei has been established with no mishap. And now it is time for Showa Senbei to begin its full-fledged business activities.

Going forward, we will look at the following 16 business activities in the same format.

1. Borrow money
2. Purchase fixed assets
3. Procure raw materials
4. Hire production workers and record as direct labor costs
5. Pay payroll-related expenses
6. Book depreciation and manufacturing overheads
7. Book depreciation and SG&A expenses
8. Pay for the raw materials
9. Ship products
10. Collect cash
11. Write-off cost
12. Pay interest
13. Repay debt (Pay principal)
14. Clear inventory
15. Book income tax
16. Declare dividend and pay

無事に「昭和せんべい」は設立されました。それでは，本格的な事業活動を始めていきます。

　この後は以下の16の事業活動を同じフォーマットで順に見ていきます。

1. お金を借りる
2. 固定資産を購入する
3. 材料を調達する
4. 作業者を雇用し直接人件費を計上する
5. 給与関連費用を支払う
6. 減価償却費と製造間接費を計上する
7. 減価償却費と販管費を計上する
8. 材料費を支払う
9. 製品を出荷する
10. 代金を回収する
11. 貸倒れが発生する
12. 利息を支払う
13. 借入金（元本）を返済する
14. 在庫を整理する
15. 税金を計上する
16. 配当を支払う

1 Borrow Money

Although you have provided some money, Showa Senbei's capital is still insufficient to start business operation. So, it decides to borrow $200,000 from a bank. The annual interest rate is set at 5% with yearly repayment of $50,000. (The principal payment will be fulfilled in 4 years.)

● Debt increases in the CFS (A).

● Cash increases in the asset section in the BS (B).

● The $50,000 to be repaid in the first year is recorded as the current portion of debt in the BS (C), and the remaining $150,000 is listed as long-term debts because it will be repaid in the subsequent years (D).

Since interest is not paid at the time of borrowing, do not record anything for interests paid at this stage.

Income Statement	損益計算書	Foundation 設立	Act.1 活動1	After 1 活動1後
Sales (Revenue)	売上高（営業収益）			0
− Cost of Goods Sold	売上原価			0
= Gross Margin	売上総利益	0	0	0
− Selling, General & Administrative Expenses	販管費			0
= Income from Operations	営業利益	0	0	0
+/− Non-operating Profit/Expenses	営業外損益			0
− Income Taxes	法人所得税等			0
= Net Income	当期純利益	0	0	0

Cash Flow Statement	キャッシュフロー計算書	Foundation 設立	Act.1 活動1	After 1 活動1後
Cash Receipts from Customers	売上収入			0
− Cash Paid to Suppliers and Employees	経費の支払いによる支出			0
− Income Taxes Paid	法人所得税等の支払い			0
=A Cash Flows from Operating Activities	営業活動によるキャッシュフロー	0	0	0
− Purchase of Property, Plant & Equipment	固定資産の取得			0
− Purchase of Marketable Securities	金融資産の取得			0
=B Cash Flows from Investing Activities	投資活動によるキャッシュフロー	0	0	0
Increase in Debt	借入金・社債の増加		200,000	200,000
− Interests Paid	利息支払い	A		0
− Dividends Paid	配当支払い			0
+ Issuance of Common Stock	株式の発行	100,000	0	100,000
=C Cash Flows from Financing Activities	財務活動によるキャッシュフロー	100,000	200,000	300,000
A+B+C Change in Cash	現金の増減額	100,000	200,000	300,000

あなたが出資をしたものの,「昭和せんべい」が事業活動を行うためにはまだ資金が不足しています。そこで銀行から 200,000 ドルを借り入れることにしました。金利は年 5%であり,毎年 50,000 ドルずつ元本を返済します（4 年間で全額返済するということです）。

● CFS 上で借入金・社債が増加します（A）。
● BS の資産で現金が増加します（B）。
● 1 年目に返済予定の分 50,000 ドルは,BS の短期社債・借入金として計上し（C),残りの 150,000 ドルは返済までの期間が 1 年以上なので BS の長期社債・借入金として計上します（D）。

なお,支払い利息は借り入れ時点で払う必要はないので,この段階では財務三表に変化は与えません。

	Balance Sheet	貸借対照表	Foundation 設立	Act.1 活動1	After 1 活動1後
	Cash	現金	100,000	200,000	300,000
+	Marketable Securities	金融資産（有価証券）		B	0
+	Accounts Receivable	売上債権（売掛金）			0
+	Inventories	棚卸資産（在庫）			0
+	Prepaid Expenses	前払費用			0
+	Other Current Assets	その他流動資産			0
=	Current Assets	流動資産	100,000	200,000	300,000
+	Property, Plant & Equipment	有形固定資産			0
+	Financial Investment	金融投資			0
+	Other Fixed Assets	その他固定資産			0
=	Total Assets	資産合計	100,000	200,000	300,000
	Accounts Payable	仕入債務（買掛金）			0
+	Accrued Expenses	未払費用			0
+	Income Taxes Payable	未払法人所得税			0
+	Advanced Payment	前受金			0
+	Current Portion of Debt	短期社債・借入金		C 50,000	50,000
+	Other Current Liabilities	その他流動負債			0
=a	Current Liabilities	流動負債	0	50,000	50,000
	Long-term Debt	長期社債・借入金		D 150,000	150,000
+	Other Fixed Liabilities	その他固定負債			0
=b	Fixed Liabilities	固定負債	0	150,000	150,000
a+b=c	Total Liabilities	負債合計	0	200,000	200,000
	Capital Stock	資本金	100,000	0	100,000
+	Retained Earnings	利益剰余金			0
=d	Shareholders' Equity	株主資本合計	100,000	0	100,000
c+d	Total Liabilities & Equity	負債及び資本合計	100,000	200,000	300,000

Activity 1: Application Exercise

Showa Senbei decides to borrow $300,000 with a yearly interest rate of 6% per year. The $300,000 will be repaid in one lump sum in 6 years.

How do the financial statements change? Note that all principal payments will be made 6 years from today.

Income Statement	損益計算書	1 Exercise 1 応用問題
Sales (Revenue)	売上高（営業収益）	
− Cost of Goods Sold	売上原価	
= Gross Margin	売上総利益	0
− Selling, General & Administrative Expenses	販管費	
= Income from Operations	営業利益	0
+/− Non-operating Profit/Expenses	営業外損益	
− Income Taxes	法人所得税等	
= Net Income	当期純利益	0

Cash Flow Statement	キャッシュフロー計算書	1 Exercise 1 応用問題
Cash Receipts from Customers	売上収入	
− Cash Paid to Suppliers and Employees	経費の支払いによる支出	
− Income Taxes Paid	法人所得税等の支払い	
=A Cash Flows from Operating Activities	営業活動によるキャッシュフロー	0
− Purchase of Property, Plant & Equipment	固定資産の取得	
− Purchase of Marketable Securities	金融資産の取得	
=B Cash Flows from Investing Activities	投資活動によるキャッシュフロー	0
Increase in Debt	借入金・社債の増加	300,000
− Interests Paid	利息支払い	
− Dividends Paid	配当支払い	
+ Issuance of Common Stock	株式の発行	0
=C Cash Flows from Financing Activities	財務活動によるキャッシュフロー	300,000
A+B+C Change in Cash	現金の増減額	300,000

Repayment is 6 years from now, so the full amount of the loan will be recorded as long-term debt.

銀行から年 6％の金利を支払う条件で 300,000 ドルの借り入れを行います。返済は 6 年後に一括で行います。

財務三表はどのように変化しますか？　元本の返済はすべて 6 年後であることに注意してください。

	Balance Sheet	貸借対照表	1 Exercise 1 応用問題
	Cash	現金	300,000
+	Marketable Securities	金融資産（有価証券）	
+	Accounts Receivable	売上債権（売掛金）	
+	Inventories	棚卸資産（在庫）	
+	Prepaid Expenses	前払費用	
+	Other Current Assets	その他流動資産	
=	Current Assets	流動資産	300,000
+	Property, Plant & Equipment	有形固定資産	
+	Financial Investment	金融投資	
+	Other Fixed Assets	その他固定資産	
=	Total Assets	資産合計	300,000
	Accounts Payable	仕入債務（買掛金）	
+	Accrued Expenses	未払費用	
+	Income Taxes Payable	未払法人所得税	
+	Advanced Payment	前受金	
+	Current Portion of Debt	短期社債・借入金	
+	Other Current Liabilities	その他流動負債	
=a	Current Liabilities	流動負債	0
	Long-term Debt	長期社債・借入金	300,000
+	Other Fixed Liabilities	その他固定負債	
=b	Fixed Liabilities	固定負債	300,000
a+b=c	Total Liabilities	負債合計	300,000
	Capital Stock	資本金	0
+	Retained Earnings	利益剰余金	
=d	Shareholders' Equity	株主資本合計	0
c+d	Total Liabilities & Equity	負債及び資本合計	300,000

返済は 6 年後なので借入れの全額が長期社債・借入金に計上されます。

Activity

2 Purchase Fixed Assets

Showa Senbei purchases land and builds a factory and office to produce, distribute, and sell senbei. Factory construction also includes senbei manufacturing equipment. The total expenditure is $175,000 and is paid in cash.

Land, buildings, and equipment are fixed assets that are recorded on the BS, however, they are not expensed at this stage. Expenses related to fixed assets are recorded as depreciation over the period of its productive life (this will be explained in detail in Activities 6 and 7).

● The Purchase of PP&E is recorded on the CFS by $175,000 to make cash payments (A).
● Cash is reduced in the BS by the same amount (B).
● PP&E in the BS increases by the purchase price for $175,000 (C).

	Income Statement	損益計算書	After 1 活動1後	Act.2 活動2	After 2 活動2後
	Sales (Revenue)	売上高（営業収益）	0		0
–	Cost of Goods Sold	売上原価	0		0
=	Gross Margin	売上総利益	0	0	0
–	Selling, General & Administrative Expenses	販管費	0		0
=	Income from Operations	営業利益	0	0	0
+/–	Non-operating Profit/Expenses	営業外損益	0		0
–	Income Taxes	法人所得税等	0		0
=	Net Income	当期純利益	0	0	0

	Cash Flow Statement	キャッシュフロー計算書	After 1 活動1後	Act.2 活動2	After 2 活動2後
	Cash Receipts from Customers	売上収入	0		0
–	Cash Paid to Suppliers and Employees	経費の支払いによる支出	0		0
–	Income Taxes Paid	法人所得税等の支払い	0		0
=A	Cash Flows from Operating Activities	営業活動によるキャッシュフロー	0	0	0
–	Purchase of Property, Plant & Equipment	固定資産の取得	0	A 175,000	175,000
–	Purchase of Marketable Securities	金融資産の取得	0		0
=B	Cash Flows from Investing Activities	投資活動によるキャッシュフロー	0	–175,000	–175,000
	Increase in Debt	借入金・社債の増加	200,000		200,000
–	Interests Paid	利息支払い	0		0
–	Dividends Paid	配当支払い	0		0
+	Issuance of Common Stock	株式の発行	100,000		100,000
=C	Cash Flows from Financing Activities	財務活動によるキャッシュフロー	300,000	0	300,000
A+B+C	Change in Cash	現金の増減額	300,000	–175,000	125,000

固定資産を購入する

　せんべいを作り販売するために土地を購入し，工場施設と本社としての事務所を建設します。工場建設にはせんべいの製造設備の導入も含まれます。取得金額の合計は 175,000 ドルであり，現金で支払います。

　土地・建物・設備は固定資産であり，これらの金額は BS に記録され，この段階では費用計上はされません。固定資産に関わる費用は，その稼働期間にわたって取得価格の一部を減価償却費（活動 6，7 にて詳述します）として計上していきます。

● 現金支払いを行うため，CFS 上の固定資産の取得で 175,000 ドルが計上されます（A）。

● その分 BS の現金残高が減少します（B）。

● BS の固定資産が 175,000 ドル増加します（C）。

	Balance Sheet	貸借対照表	After 1 活動1後	Act.2 活動2	After 2 活動2後
	Cash	現金	300,000	−175,000	125,000
+	Marketable Securities	金融資産（有価証券）	0 B		0
+	Accounts Receivable	売上債権（売掛金）	0		0
+	Inventories	棚卸資産（在庫）	0		0
+	Prepaid Expenses	前払費用	0		0
+	Other Current Assets	その他流動資産	0		0
=	Current Assets	流動資産	300,000	−175,000	125,000
+	Property, Plant & Equipment	有形固定資産	0 C	175,000	175,000
+	Financial Investment	金融投資	0		0
+	Other Fixed Assets	その他固定資産	0		0
=	Total Assets	資産合計	300,000	0	300,000
	Accounts Payable	仕入債務（買掛金）	0		0
+	Accrued Expenses	未払費用	0		0
+	Income Taxes Payable	未払法人所得税	0		0
+	Advanced Payment	前受金	0		0
+	Current Portion of Debt	短期社債・借入金	50,000		50,000
+	Other Current Liabilities	その他流動負債	0		0
=a	Current Liabilities	流動負債	50,000	0	50,000
	Long-term Debt	長期社債・借入金	150,000		150,000
+	Other Fixed Liabilities	その他固定負債	0		0
=b	Fixed Liabilities	固定負債	150,000	0	150,000
a+b=c	Total Liabilities	負債合計	200,000	0	200,000
	Capital Stock	資本金	100,000	0	100,000
+	Retained Earnings	利益剰余金	0		0
=d	Shareholders' Equity	株主資本合計	100,000	0	100,000
c+d	Total Liabilities & Equity	負債及び資本合計	300,000	0	300,000

Showa Senbei is making another purchase in PP&E. Below are two different ways they can make this purchase.

A. Buy a $22,000 delivery truck in cash.

B. Buy a $22,000 delivery truck with on credit.

How do the financial statements change in A and B, respectively?

Income Statement	損益計算書	2 Exercise A 2 応用問題 A	2 Exercise B 2 応用問題 B
Sales (Revenue)	売上高（営業収益）		
− Cost of Goods Sold	売上原価		
= Gross Margin	売上総利益	0	0
− Selling, General & Administrative Expenses	販管費		
= Income from Operations	営業利益	0	0
+/− Non-operating Profit/Expenses	営業外損益		
− Income Taxes	法人所得税等		
= Net Income	当期純利益	0	0

Cash Flow Statement	キャッシュフロー計算書	2 Exercise A 2 応用問題 A	2 Exercise B 2 応用問題 B
Cash Receipts from Customers	売上収入		
− Cash Paid to Suppliers and Employees	経費の支払いによる支出		
− Income Taxes Paid	法人所得税等の支払い		
=A Cash Flows from Operating Activities	営業活動によるキャッシュフロー	0	0
− Purchase of Property, Plant & Equipment	固定資産の取得	22,000	
− Purchase of Marketable Securities	金融資産の取得		
=B Cash Flows from Investing Activities	投資活動によるキャッシュフロー	−22,000	0
Increase in Debt	借入金・社債の増加		
− Interests Paid	利息支払い		
− Dividends Paid	配当支払い		
+ Issuance of Common Stock	株式の発行		
=C Cash Flows from Financing Activities	財務活動によるキャッシュフロー	0	0
A+B+C Change in Cash	現金の増減額	−22,000	0

For B, the CFS remains unchanged because the cash has not yet been paid. Instead, it is considered as a liability that will be paid in the future and is recorded as accounts payable in the BS.

別の固定資産を取得するとし，以下の 2 つの支払い方法を考えます。

A. 現金で 22,000 ドルの配達用トラックを購入したとします。
B. 22,000 ドルの配達用トラックを購入しましたが，支払いは後日行うものとします。
A，B それぞれの場合，財務三表はどのように変化しますか？

	Balance Sheet	貸借対照表	2 Exercise A 2 応用問題 A	2 Exercise B 2 応用問題 B
	Cash	現金	−22,000	0
+	Marketable Securities	金融資産（有価証券）		
+	Accounts Receivable	売上債権（売掛金）		
+	Inventories	棚卸資産（在庫）		
+	Prepaid Expenses	前払費用		
+	Other Current Assets	その他流動資産		
=	Current Assets	流動資産	−22,000	0
+	Property, Plant & Equipment	有形固定資産	22,000	22,000
+	Financial Investment	金融投資		
+	Other Fixed Assets	その他固定資産		
=	Total Assets	資産合計	0	22,000
	Accounts Payable	仕入債務（買掛金）		22,000
+	Accrued Expenses	未払費用		
+	Income Taxes Payable	未払法人所得税		
+	Advanced Payment	前受金		
+	Current Portion of Debt	短期社債・借入金		
+	Other Current Liabilities	その他流動負債		
=a	Current Liabilities	流動負債	0	22,000
	Long-term Debt	長期社債・借入金		
+	Other Fixed Liabilities	その他固定負債		
=b	Fixed Liabilities	固定負債	0	0
a+b=c	Total Liabilities	負債合計	0	22,000
	Capital Stock	資本金	0	0
+	Retained Earnings	利益剰余金		
=d	Shareholders' Equity	株主資本合計	0	0
c+d	Total Liabilities & Equity	負債及び資本合計	0	22,000

　B の場合は，現金はまだ支払っていませんので CFS に変化はありません。この金額はいずれ払わなければならない債務なので，BS の仕入債務として計上します。

Activity 2: Application Exercise 2

The Company decides to purchase a short-term treasury bill (the bond matures within a year) for $5,000, with cash that has no use for the time being.

How do the financial statements change?

Income Statement	損益計算書	2 Exercise 2 2 応用問題 2
Sales (Revenue)	売上高（営業収益）	
− Cost of Goods Sold	売上原価	
= Gross Margin	売上総利益	0
− Selling, General & Administrative Expenses	販管費	
= Income from Operations	営業利益	0
+/− Non-operating Profit/Expenses	営業外損益	
− Income Taxes	法人所得税等	
= Net Income	当期純利益	0

Cash Flow Statement	キャッシュフロー計算書	2 Exercise 2 2 応用問題 2
Cash Receipts from Customers	売上収入	
− Cash Paid to Suppliers and Employees	経費の支払いによる支出	
− Income Taxes Paid	法人所得税等の支払い	
=A Cash Flows from Operating Activities	営業活動によるキャッシュフロー	0
− Purchase of Property, Plant & Equipment	固定資産の取得	
− Purchase of Marketable Securities	金融資産の取得	5,000
=B Cash Flows from Investing Activities	投資活動によるキャッシュフロー	−5,000
Increase in Debt	借入金・社債の増加	
− Interests Paid	利息支払い	
− Dividends Paid	配当支払い	
+ Issuance of Common Stock	株式の発行	
=C Cash Flows from Financing Activities	財務活動によるキャッシュフロー	0
A+B+C Change in Cash	現金の増減額	−5,000

Because the bond matures within 1 year it is recorded as a marketable security. If the bond is a long-term investment, it is recorded as a financial investment.

当面使用する見込みのない現金を活用するために短期国債（1 年以内に満期が来るもの）を 5,000 ドルで購入するとします。

財務三表はどのように変化しますか？

Balance Sheet	貸借対照表	2 Exercise 2 2 応用問題 2
Cash	現金	−5,000
+ Marketable Securities	金融資産（有価証券）	5,000
+ Accounts Receivable	売上債権（売掛金）	
+ Inventories	棚卸資産（在庫）	
+ Prepaid Expenses	前払費用	
+ Other Current Assets	その他流動資産	
= Current Assets	流動資産	0
+ Property, Plant & Equipment	有形固定資産	
+ Financial Investment	金融投資	
+ Other Fixed Assets	その他固定資産	
= Total Assets	資産合計	0
Accounts Payable	仕入債務（買掛金）	
+ Accrued Expenses	未払費用	
+ Income Taxes Payable	未払法人所得税	
+ Advanced Payment	前受金	
+ Current Portion of Debt	短期社債・借入金	
+ Other Current Liabilities	その他流動負債	
=a Current Liabilities	流動負債	0
Long-term Debt	長期社債・借入金	
+ Other Fixed Liabilities	その他固定負債	
=b Fixed Liabilities	固定負債	0
a+b=c Total Liabilities	負債合計	0
Capital Stock	資本金	0
+ Retained Earnings	利益剰余金	
=d Shareholders' Equity	株主資本合計	0
c+d Total Liabilities & Equity	負債及び資本合計	0

1 年以内に満期が来る金融資産なので流動資産になります。もし長期的な投資資産であるならば，固定資産の金融投資となります。

Activity

3 Procure Raw Materials

Showa Senbei purchases a total of $80,000 worth of raw materials (rice, soy sauce), in addition to packaging materials to produce and sell senbei. This purchase is made on credit so the cash transaction occurs at a later date.

- Materials are considered as inventory, so inventories in the BS increases by $80,000 (A).
- The accounts payable in the BS increases by the value of the materials received (B).

Income Statement	損益計算書	After 2 活動2後	Act.3 活動3	After 3 活動3後
Sales (Revenue)	売上高（営業収益）	0		0
− Cost of Goods Sold	売上原価	0		0
= Gross Margin	売上総利益	0	0	0
− Selling, General & Administrative Expenses	販管費	0		0
= Income from Operations	営業利益	0	0	0
+/− Non-operating Profit/Expenses	営業外損益	0		0
− Income Taxes	法人所得税等	0		0
= Net Income	当期純利益	0	0	0

Cash Flow Statement	キャッシュフロー計算書	After 2 活動2後	Act.3 活動3	After 3 活動3後
Cash Receipts from Customers	売上収入	0		0
− Cash Paid to Suppliers and Employees	経費の支払いによる支出	0		0
− Income Taxes Paid	法人所得税等の支払い	0		0
=A Cash Flows from Operating Activities	営業活動によるキャッシュフロー	0	0	0
− Purchase of Property, Plant & Equipment	固定資産の取得	175,000		175,000
− Purchase of Marketable Securities	金融資産の取得	0		0
=B Cash Flows from Investing Activities	投資活動によるキャッシュフロー	−175,000	0	−175,000
Increase in Debt	借入金・社債の増加	200,000		200,000
− Interests Paid	利息支払い	0		0
− Dividends Paid	配当支払い	0		0
+ Issuance of Common Stock	株式の発行	100,000		100,000
=C Cash Flows from Financing Activities	財務活動によるキャッシュフロー	300,000	0	300,000
A+B+C Change in Cash	現金の増減額	125,000	0	125,000

③ 材料を調達する

　せんべいを生産し販売するために必要な原材料（米，醤油）や包装資材を合計で 80,000 ドル分仕入れました。仕入れは掛けで行われ，仕入先（サプライヤー）への現金の支払いは後日になります。

● 材料は棚卸資産に含まれるので BS の棚卸資産が 80,000 ドル増加します（A）。

● BS の仕入債務がその分増加します（B）。

	Balance Sheet	貸借対照表	After 2 活動2後	Act.3 活動3	After 3 活動3後
	Cash	現金	125,000	0	125,000
+	Marketable Securities	金融資産（有価証券）	0		0
+	Accounts Receivable	売上債権（売掛金）	0		0
+	Inventories	棚卸資産（在庫）	0	A 80,000	80,000
+	Prepaid Expenses	前払費用	0		0
+	Other Current Assets	その他流動資産	0		0
=	Current Assets	流動資産	125,000	80,000	205,000
+	Property, Plant & Equipment	有形固定資産	175,000	0	175,000
+	Financial Investment	金融投資	0		0
+	Other Fixed Assets	その他固定資産	0		0
=	Total Assets	資産合計	300,000	80,000	380,000
	Accounts Payable	仕入債務（買掛金）	0	B 80,000	80,000
+	Accrued Expenses	未払費用	0		0
+	Income Taxes Payable	未払法人所得税	0		0
+	Advanced Payment	前受金	0		0
+	Current Portion of Debt	短期社債・借入金	50,000		50,000
+	Other Current Liabilities	その他流動負債	0		0
=a	Current Liabilities	流動負債	50,000	80,000	130,000
	Long-term Debt	長期社債・借入金	150,000		150,000
+	Other Fixed Liabilities	その他固定負債	0		0
=b	Fixed Liabilities	固定負債	150,000	0	150,000
a+b=c	Total Liabilities	負債合計	200,000	80,000	280,000
	Capital Stock	資本金	100,000	0	100,000
+	Retained Earnings	利益剰余金	0		0
=d	Shareholders' Equity	株主資本合計	100,000	0	100,000
c+d	Total Liabilities & Equity	負債及び資本合計	300,000	80,000	380,000

The rice supplier offered a special discount for an immediate cash payment, allowing Showa Senbei to purchase and receive $10,000 (after discount) worth of rice and pays cash in exchange for it.

How do the financial statements change?

	Income Statement	損益計算書	3 Exercise 3 応用問題
	Sales (Revenue)	売上高（営業収益）	
−	Cost of Goods Sold	売上原価	
=	Gross Margin	売上総利益	0
−	Selling, General & Administrative Expenses	販管費	
=	Income from Operations	営業利益	0
+/−	Non-operating Profit/Expenses	営業外損益	
−	Income Taxes	法人所得税等	
=	Net Income	当期純利益	0

	Cash Flow Statement	キャッシュフロー計算書	3 Exercise 3 応用問題
	Cash Receipts from Customers	売上収入	
−	Cash Paid to Suppliers and Employees	経費の支払いによる支出	10,000
−	Income Taxes Paid	法人所得税等の支払い	
=A	Cash Flows from Operating Activities	営業活動によるキャッシュフロー	−10,000
−	Purchase of Property, Plant & Equipment	固定資産の取得	
−	Purchase of Marketable Securities	金融資産の取得	
=B	Cash Flows from Investing Activities	投資活動によるキャッシュフロー	0
	Increase in Debt	借入金・社債の増加	
−	Interests Paid	利息支払い	
−	Dividends Paid	配当支払い	
+	Issuance of Common Stock	株式の発行	
=C	Cash Flows from Financing Activities	財務活動によるキャッシュフロー	0
A+B+C	Change in Cash	現金の増減額	−10,000

Procuring raw materials does not affect the IS even though cash is paid.

　お米の仕入先が，現金支払いを行うことを条件に，特別な値引きをすることを打診してきたので，購入することにしました。10,000 ドル（値引き後）分のお米を受け取り，同時に現金を支払います。

　財務三表はどのように変化しますか？

	Balance Sheet	貸借対照表	3 Exercise 3 応用問題
	Cash	現金	−10,000
+	Marketable Securities	金融資産（有価証券）	
+	Accounts Receivable	売上債権（売掛金）	
+	Inventories	棚卸資産（在庫）	10,000
+	Prepaid Expenses	前払費用	
+	Other Current Assets	その他流動資産	
=	Current Assets	流動資産	0
+	Property, Plant & Equipment	有形固定資産	0
+	Financial Investment	金融投資	
+	Other Fixed Assets	その他固定資産	
=	Total Assets	資産合計	0
	Accounts Payable	仕入債務（買掛金）	
+	Accrued Expenses	未払費用	
+	Income Taxes Payable	未払法人所得税	
+	Advanced Payment	前受金	
+	Current Portion of Debt	短期社債・借入金	
+	Other Current Liabilities	その他流動負債	
=a	Current Liabilities	流動負債	0
	Long-term Debt	長期社債・借入金	
+	Other Fixed Liabilities	その他固定負債	
=b	Fixed Liabilities	固定負債	0
a+b=c	Total Liabilities	負債合計	0
	Capital Stock	資本金	0
+	Retained Earnings	利益剰余金	
=d	Shareholders' Equity	株主資本合計	0
c+d	Total Liabilities & Equity	負債及び資本合計	0

　現金支払いがあったとしても原材料の仕入れは PL に影響を与えません。

⟨4⟩ Hire Production Workers and Record as Direct Labor Costs

One-point Lecture · Labor Cost

In general, employees must bear social security fees and income taxes (including inhabitant tax). Those will be kept by the company and paid to the government directly at a later date.

Additionally, the social security fees are split evenly the between the employees and the employing company.

Showa Senbei is obligated to pay $30,000 as a worker's salary. Out of this $30,000, 15% ($4,500) is withheld as a social security fee and 10% ($3,000) is withheld as income tax. Therefore, the remaining $22,500 is paid to the employee as a take-home salary.

The company pays the same amount of social security fees as the employee, so the total salary-related expenses are $30,000 plus the $4,500, totaling $34,500.

Salary-related Expenses of Showa Senbei

	Pay to Worker	To Others	Total
Salary	30,000	0	30,000
Social Security (Employer)	−4,500	4,500	0
Withholding Tax	−3,000	3,000	0
Social Security (Employee)		4,500	4,500
Total	**22,500**	**12,000**	**34,500**

ワンポイント関連講義　人件費

　一般に，企業に雇用される従業員は，社会保険料と所得税（住民税を含む）を負担する必要があります。これらの負担額は会社によって源泉徴収され，後日会社から直接政府に支払われます。

　また，社会保険料は，従業員と雇用主である会社とで折半され，従業員と会社が同額を負担します。

　「昭和せんべい」の場合，労働者の給料の額面は 30,000 ドルだとします。このうち，15%の 4,500 ドルが社会保険料，10%の 3,000 ドルが所得税として源泉徴収されます。そのため給与として従業員に支払われる手取り額は残りの 22,500 ドルです。

　会社は従業員と同額の社会保険料を負担するので，給与関連全体の費用は 30,000 ドルに会社負担分の社会保険料 4,500 ドルを加えた 34,500 ドルとなります。

「昭和せんべい」の給与関連費用

	従業員への支払い額	その他	合計
給与	30,000	0	30,000
社会保険料（従業員負担分）	−4,500	4,500	0
源泉徴収税額	−3,000	3,000	0
社会保険料（会社負担分）		4,500	4,500
人件費総額	**22,500**	**12,000**	**34,500**

Showa Senbei hires a worker on a salary of $30,000 to produce senbei. The total salary-related expenses for the worker is $34,500, as seen on the previous page, of which $22,500 will be paid to the worker, and the remaining $12,000 to the government in the future.

● $22,500 is recorded as cash paid to suppliers and employees in the CFS (A).
● This reduces the cash balance in the BS (B).
● The $12,000 that the company will pay to the government in the future is booked as an accrued expense in the BS (C) (for your reference, please note that the actual BS uses a different item called "Deposit" frequently).
● These costs are directly related to the production of rice crackers and increase the value of inventories in the BS by $34,500 (D).

Income Statement	損益計算書	After 3 活動3後	Act.4 活動4	After 4 活動4後
Sales (Revenue)	売上高 (営業収益)	0		0
− Cost of Goods Sold	売上原価	0		0
= Gross Margin	売上総利益	0	0	0
− Selling, General & Administrative Expenses	販管費	0		0
= Income from Operations	営業利益	0	0	0
+/− Non-operating Profit/Expenses	営業外損益	0		0
− Income Taxes	法人所得税等	0		0
= Net Income	当期純利益	0	0	0

Cash Flow Statement	キャッシュフロー計算書	After 3 活動3後	Act.4 活動4	After 4 活動4後
Cash Receipts from Customers	売上収入	0		0
− Cash Paid to Suppliers and Employees	経費の支払いによる支出	0	A 22,500	22,500
− Income Taxes Paid	法人所得税等の支払い	0		0
=A Cash Flows from Operating Activities	営業活動によるキャッシュフロー	0	−22,500	−22,500
− Purchase of Property, Plant & Equipment	固定資産の取得	175,000		175,000
− Purchase of Marketable Securities	金融資産の取得	0		0
=B Cash Flows from Investing Activities	投資活動によるキャッシュフロー	−175,000	0	−175,000
Increase in Debt	借入金・社債の増加	200,000		200,000
− Interests Paid	利息支払い	0		0
− Dividends Paid	配当支払い	0		0
+ Issuance of Common Stock	株式の発行	100,000		100,000
=C Cash Flows from Financing Activities	財務活動によるキャッシュフロー	300,000	0	300,000
A+B+C Change in Cash	現金の増減額	125,000	−22,500	102,500

せんべいを生産するために 30,000 ドルの給与で作業者を雇用します。この従業員に関する「昭和せんべい」の給与関連の総費用は前ページで見た通り 34,500 ドルとなり，そのうち手取り給与の 22,500 ドルが支払われ，残りの 12,000 ドルは後日政府に支払われます。

● 22,500 ドルは CFS の経費の支払いによる支出に当たります（A）。
● これにより BS の現金残高が減少します（B）。
● 後に会社から政府に支払われる予定の 12,000 ドルは BS の未払費用として計上されます（C）（なお，実際の BS には「預り金」という項目が使用されます）。

● これらのコストは，せんべいの生産に直接的に関係しており，棚卸資産の価値を増加させるので，BS の棚卸資産の価値が 34,500 ドル増加します（D）。

	Balance Sheet	貸借対照表	After 3 活動3後	Act.4 活動4	After 4 活動4後
	Cash	現金	125,000	B 22,500	102,500
+	Marketable Securities	金融資産（有価証券）	0		0
+	Accounts Receivable	売上債権（売掛金）	0		0
+	Inventories	棚卸資産（在庫）	80,000	D 34,500	114,500
+	Prepaid Expenses	前払費用	0		0
+	Other Current Assets	その他流動資産	0		0
=	Current Assets	流動資産	205,000	12,000	217,000
+	Property, Plant & Equipment	有形固定資産	175,000	0	175,000
+	Financial Investment	金融投資	0		0
+	Other Fixed Assets	その他固定資産	0		0
=	Total Assets	資産合計	380,000	12,000	392,000
	Accounts Payable	仕入債務（買掛金）	80,000	0	80,000
+	Accrued Expenses	未払費用	0	C 12,000	12,000
+	Income Taxes Payable	未払法人所得税	0		0
+	Advanced Payment	前受金	0		0
+	Current Portion of Debt	短期社債・借入金	50,000		50,000
+	Other Current Liabilities	その他流動負債	0		0
=a	Current Liabilities	流動負債	130,000	12,000	142,000
	Long-term Debt	長期社債・借入金	150,000		150,000
+	Other Fixed Liabilities	その他固定負債	0		0
=b	Fixed Liabilities	固定負債	150,000	0	150,000
a+b=c	Total Liabilities	負債合計	280,000	12,000	292,000
	Capital Stock	資本金	100,000	0	100,000
+	Retained Earnings	利益剰余金	0	0	0
=d	Shareholders' Equity	株主資本合計	100,000	0	100,000
c+d	Total Liabilities & Equity	負債及び資本合計	380,000	12,000	392,000

5 Pay Payroll-related Expenses

It is time for Showa Senbei to pay the government $12,000 of salary-related expenses accrued in Activity 4.

- $12,000 is booked as cash paid to suppliers and employees in the CFS (A).
- Cash balance decreases in the BS (B).
- By making the payment, the unpaid accrued expense that is part of liabilities on the BS disappears (C).

Note that paying accrued expenses does not affect the IS.

Income Statement	損益計算書	After 4 活動4後	Act.5 活動5	After 5 活動5後
Sales (Revenue)	売上高（営業収益）	0		0
− Cost of Goods Sold	売上原価	0		0
= Gross Margin	売上総利益	0	0	0
− Selling, General & Administrative Expenses	販管費	0		0
= Income from Operations	営業利益	0	0	0
+/− Non-operating Profit/Expenses	営業外損益	0		0
− Income Taxes	法人所得税等	0		0
= Net Income	当期純利益	0	0	0

Cash Flow Statement	キャッシュフロー計算書	After 4 活動4後	Act.5 活動5	After 5 活動5後
Cash Receipts from Customers	売上収入	0		0
− Cash Paid to Suppliers and Employees	経費の支払いによる支出	22,500	A 12,000	34,500
− Income Taxes Paid	法人所得税等の支払い	0		0
=A Cash Flows from Operating Activities	営業活動によるキャッシュフロー	−22,500	−12,000	−34,500
− Purchase of Property, Plant & Equipment	固定資産の取得	175,000		175,000
− Purchase of Marketable Securities	金融資産の取得	0		0
=B Cash Flows from Investing Activities	投資活動によるキャッシュフロー	−175,000	0	−175,000
Increase in Debt	借入金・社債の増加	200,000		200,000
− Interests Paid	利息支払い	0		0
− Dividends Paid	配当支払い	0		0
+ Issuance of Common Stock	株式の発行	100,000		100,000
=C Cash Flows from Financing Activities	財務活動によるキャッシュフロー	300,000	0	300,000
A+B+C Change in Cash	現金の増減額	102,500	−12,000	90,500

活動
5 給与関連費用を支払う

活動4で計上された給与関連費用12,000ドルを政府に支払う時期が来ました。

- CFSの経費の支払いによる支出に12,000ドルが計上されます（A）。
- BSの現金残高が減少します（B）。
- 支払いを行うことでBSの負債の一部である未払費用がなくなります（C）。

なお，未払費用を支払うことはPLに影響を与えません。

Balance Sheet	貸借対照表	After 4 活動4後	Act.5 活動5	After 5 活動5後
Cash	現金	102,500	B −12,000	90,500
+ Marketable Securities	金融資産（有価証券）	0		0
+ Accounts Receivable	売上債権（売掛金）	0		0
+ Inventories	棚卸資産（在庫）	114,500	0	114,500
+ Prepaid Expenses	前払費用	0		0
+ Other Current Assets	その他流動資産	0		0
= Current Assets	流動資産	217,000	−12,000	205,000
+ Property, Plant & Equipment	有形固定資産	175,000		175,000
+ Financial Investment	金融投資	0		0
+ Other Fixed Assets	その他固定資産	0		0
= Total Assets	資産合計	392,000	−12,000	380,000
Accounts Payable	仕入債務（買掛金）	80,000		80,000
+ Accrued Expenses	未払費用	12,000	C −12,000	0
+ Income Taxes Payable	未払法人所得税	0		0
+ Advanced Payment	前受金	0		0
+ Current Portion of Debt	短期社債・借入金	50,000		50,000
+ Other Current Liabilities	その他流動負債	0		0
=a Current Liabilities	流動負債	142,000	−12,000	130,000
Long-term Debt	長期社債・借入金	150,000		150,000
+ Other Fixed Liabilities	その他固定負債	0		0
=b Fixed Liabilities	固定負債	150,000	0	150,000
a+b=c Total Liabilities	負債合計	292,000	−12,000	280,000
Capital Stock	資本金	100,000	0	100,000
+ Retained Earnings	利益剰余金	0		0
=d Shareholders' Equity	株主資本合計	100,000	0	100,000
c+d Total Liabilities & Equity	負債及び資本合計	392,000	−12,000	380,000

Activities 4, 5: Application Exercise

Suppose that a researcher is hired to create a better recipe for senbei.

A. First, record their salary of $3,520 in take-home pay for the first month. Keep in mind, the remaining $1,785 of the salary-related expenses are paid to the government at a later date.

B. At the end of the month, pay the government the remaining obligation resulting from the payroll in A.

How do the financial statements change in A and B, respectively?

(Hint: R&D expenses are SG&A expenses)

Income Statement	損益計算書	4, 5 Exercise A 4, 5 応用問題 A	4, 5 Exercise B 4, 5 応用問題 B
Sales (Revenue)	売上高（営業収益）		
− Cost of Goods Sold	売上原価		
= Gross Margin	売上総利益	0	0
− Selling, General & Administrative Expenses	販管費	5,305	
= Income from Operations	営業利益	−5,305	0
+/− Non-operating Profit/Expenses	営業外損益		
− Income Taxes	法人所得税等		
= Net Income	当期純利益	−5,305	0

Cash Flow Statement	キャッシュフロー計算書	4, 5 Exercise A 4, 5 応用問題 A	4, 5 Exercise B 4, 5 応用問題 B
Cash Receipts from Customers	売上収入		
− Cash Paid to Suppliers and Employees	経費の支払いによる支出	3,520	1,785
− Income Taxes Paid	法人所得税等の支払い		
=A Cash Flows from Operating Activities	営業活動によるキャッシュフロー	−3,520	−1,785
− Purchase of Property, Plant & Equipment	固定資産の取得		
− Purchase of Marketable Securities	金融資産の取得		
=B Cash Flows from Investing Activities	投資活動によるキャッシュフロー	0	0
Increase in Debt	借入金・社債の増加		
− Interests Paid	利息支払い		
− Dividends Paid	配当支払い		
+ Issuance of Common Stock	株式の発行		
=C Cash Flows from Financing Activities	財務活動によるキャッシュフロー	0	0
A+B+C Change in Cash	現金の増減額	−3,520	−1,785

Expenses related to research and development is directly accounted for as SG&A expenses in the IS.

「昭和せんべい」はせんべいの味の改良のために研究員を雇うとします。

A. 1 カ月分の給与を計上します。手取り金額は 3,520 ドル，政府に後日支払う関連費用は 1,785 ドルです。

B. 月末に，A の給与計算に起因する政府への支払い分を支払います。

A，B それぞれで，財務三表はどのように変化しますか？
（ヒント：研究開発費は販管費です）

Balance Sheet	貸借対照表	4, 5 Exercise A 4, 5 応用問題 A	4, 5 Exercise B 4, 5 応用問題 B
Cash	現金	−3,520	−1,785
+ Marketable Securities	金融資産（有価証券）		
+ Accounts Receivable	売上債権（売掛金）		
+ Inventories	棚卸資産（在庫）		0
+ Prepaid Expenses	前払費用		
+ Other Current Assets	その他流動資産		
= Current Assets	流動資産	−3,520	−1,785
+ Property, Plant & Equipment	有形固定資産	0	
+ Financial Investment	金融投資		
+ Other Fixed Assets	その他固定資産		
= Total Assets	資産合計	−3,520	−1,785
Accounts Payable	仕入債務（買掛金）	0	
+ Accrued Expenses	未払費用	1,785	−1,785
+ Income Taxes Payable	未払法人所得税		
+ Advanced Payment	前受金		
+ Current Portion of Debt	短期社債・借入金		
+ Other Current Liabilities	その他流動負債		
=a Current Liabilities	流動負債	1,785	−1,785
Long-term Debt	長期社債・借入金		
+ Other Fixed Liabilities	その他固定負債		
=b Fixed Liabilities	固定負債	0	0
a+b=c Total Liabilities	負債合計	1,785	−1,785
Capital Stock	資本金	0	0
+ Retained Earnings	利益剰余金	−5,305	
=d Shareholders' Equity	株主資本合計	−5,305	0
c+d Total Liabilities & Equity	負債及び資本合計	−3,520	−1,785

研究開発にかかわる費用は直接 PL の販管費として計上されます。

Activity 6 Book Depreciation and Manufacturing Overheads

One-point Lecture   Manufacturing Overhead

In order to make a product, a company must consider the various costs associated with the product, not only raw materials and labor on the production line. It requires the cost of manufacturing equipment, electricity, gas, water, and even labor costs of the supervising manager at a factory floor.

The costs that do not go directly into the product but are needed to produce it, are referred to as manufacturing overheads. Manufacturing overheads and go into inventories in the BS, just like materials. They are only recorded as the cost of goods sold in the IS when the product is shipped.

Amid manufacturing overheads, depreciation associated with fixed assets is a rather complex cost.

One-point Lecture   Depreciation

Depreciation distributes the costs of fixed assets such as plant and equipment along their functional periods (It is called amortization if the fixed assets are intangible). We allocate the depreciation cost because fixed assets are used for a long time. If you only recognize these expenses at the time of purchase, then you will make mistakes when evaluating the financial performance in each period. This cost allocation assumes that a fixed asset will become unusable from deteriorations over time. Therefore, non-deteriorating fixed assets such as land will never depreciate.

The figure on the next page provides an example of a machine costing $300,000, which works for three years. The value of the machine at the time of purchase recorded in the BS is $300,000 because the machine has not been used. After the first year of use, $100,000 will be recorded as depreciation to account for one year of deterioration. The value of the fixed asset declines and is recorded as $200,000 at the end of the first year reflecting the reduction in value caused by wear and tear (value

減価償却費と製造間接費を計上する

ワンポイント関連講義　製造間接費

　製品を作るためには，原材料費や製造ラインで作業をする労働者の人件費だけではなく，その他にもさまざまなコストがかかります。製造設備の費用，電気・ガス・水道代，また製造現場で監督・指示を行う管理者の人件費も必要です。

　このような製造に間接的にかかわるコストを製造間接費と呼びます。製造間接費は材料費などと同じく，いったん BS の棚卸資産に計上されます。その後，製品が出荷された段階で PL の売上原価に計上されます。

　製造間接費のうち，特に難しいのは，製造設備などの固定資産に関するコストである減価償却費です。

ワンポイント関連講義　減価償却費

　減価償却費は，工場や設備などの固定資産に関する費用を，それが使用できる各期間に配分するものです。固定資産は長期にわたって使用されるため，取得時に一括して費用を計上すると，各期間の業績を適切に把握できなくなってしまいます。そのため費用を減価償却費として配分するのです。この費用の配分は，固定資産の多くは時の経過や使用とともにその機能を消耗していくことを前提としています。したがって，土地のように時間の経過によって機能が変化しない資産には減価償却は行われません。

　次ページの図表の例で理解しましょう。3 年間使用する 300,000 ドルの設備を購入したとします。購入した段階では設備は使用されておらず，BS における固定資産としての残高は取得価格の 300,000 ドルです。1 年間この設備を使用すると，3 年間のうち 1 年間分の減耗が設備に生じたと考え，3 分の 1 の金額である 100,000 ドルが減価償却として計上されます。固定資産の残高は減耗分を反映し，期末の段階で 200,000 ドルとなります（価値が減るため「減価」

reduced or "depreciated"). Similarly, the next year also records depreciation of $100,000, and continues until the value of the fixed asset becomes zero at the end of the third year.

Depreciation Example

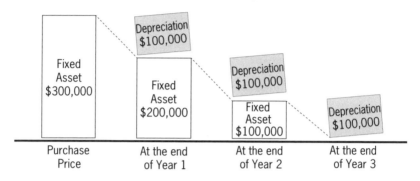

	Fixed Asset $300,000	Fixed Asset $200,000	Fixed Asset $100,000	
Depreciation		Depreciation $100,000	Depreciation $100,000	Depreciation $100,000

| Purchase | At the end | At the end | At the end |
| Price | of Year 1 | of Year 2 | of Year 3 |

Depreciation periods or depreciable life depends on the asset in question. Assets with longer functional lifetimes such as buildings (20-30 years or more) depreciate much slower than assets such as cars (5 years or so) which have much shorter functional lifetimes.

The straight-line depreciation method, as shown in the figure, takes the same amount of depreciation for each year of useful life. Alternatively, accelerated depreciation methods account for a large amount of depreciation in early years and then the depreciation value is reduced in the subsequent years. Many Japanese companies utilize the "fixed-rate method" which calculates the remaining balance of each asset multiplied by its predetermined depreciation rate. The calculation for straight-line depreciation, on the other hand, is simple. It is basically the acquisition price divided by the years of functional use.

Depreciation is an accounting process that affects the IS and the BS but does not affect cash balances or cash flow. However, when fixed assets are purchased, they do have an effect on cash balances and cash flow.

Whether depreciation is part of the manufacturing cost (COGS) or an SG&A

です）。同様に次の年も 100,000 ドルの減価償却が計上され，3 年目の期末には
固定資産の価値はゼロとなります。

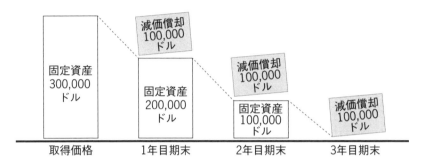

減価償却の例

資産によって減価償却の期間（耐用年数といいます）は異なります。建物の
ように長い期間使用できる資産の償却期間は長く（20 〜 30 年以上等），自動
車のような使用できる期間がより短い資産の償却期間は短く（5 年以上等）な
ります。

なお，このように毎年一定額を減価償却として計上する定額法のほかにも，
投資後早い時期に減価償却を多く計上し，その後償却負担を小さくする方法も
あります。日本企業の多くが用いる，毎年それぞれの固定資産の残高に対して
決められた一定の率（パーセント）を掛け合わせて減価償却費を算出する定率
法がこれにあたります。定額法の減価償却の計算は比較的簡単で，年間の減価
償却費は，基本的に資産の取得価格をその耐用年数で割った値となります。

減価償却費は，会計上の処理プロセスの 1 つであり，PL や BS に影響を与
えますが現金残高やキャッシュフローには影響を与えません。固定資産が購入
される時点ですでに現金残高やキャッシュフローへの影響は済んでいるからで
す。

減価償却費が製造間接費，つまり売上原価の一部となるのか，あるいは販管

expense is determined by the nature of the asset. For example, depreciation of equipment that manufactures products is a part of COGS, and depreciation of a headquarters building is accounted for as an SG&A expense.

Depreciation of Showa Senbei

Showa Senbei purchased land, buildings, and equipment for a total of $175,000 (Activity 2). The following table shows the detail.

Fixed assets and depreciation of Showa Senbei

	Purchase Price	Years of Useful Life	Annual Depreciation	Fixed Asset End of Year 1	Fixed Asset End of Year 2	Fixed Asset End of Year 3	Fixed Asset End of Year 4
Land	85,000	forever	–	85,000	85,000	85,000	85,000
Machinery	50,000	8	6,250	43,750	37,500	31,250	25,000
Office	40,000	20	2,000	38,000	36,000	34,000	32,000
Total	175,000		8,250	166,750	158,500	150,250	142,000

Showa Senbei's investment in fixed assets for $175,000 includes land for $85,000, a machinery for $50,000, and an office for $40,000. The useful life of the machinery and office are 8 years and 20 years, respectively.

The yearly depreciation for the machinery is $6,250, calculated as $50,000 divided by 8 years, and the depreciation for the office is $2,000, calculated as $40,000 divided by 20 years.

Please make sure that the value of fixed assets decreases by that amount of depreciation, and be sure to remember that there is no depreciable life associated with fixed assets such as land.

Among the fixed assets of Showa Senbei, such as land, machinery, and office, the machinery depreciation is categorized as manufacturing overheads which are applied to inventories.

On the other hand, office depreciation is classified as an SG&A expense, instead of manufacturing overhead. As a reminder, SG&A expenses are classified as period

費となるのかは，その資産の性質によって決まります。たとえば，製品を製造する設備の減価償却費は売上原価の一部となりますし，本社ビルの減価償却費は販管費として計上されます。

「昭和せんべい」の減価償却費

「昭和せんべい」は土地，建物，設備を合計 175,000 ドルで購入しました（活動 2）。以下の表は，その明細を示しています。

「昭和せんべい」の固定資産と減価償却費

	取得価格	耐用年数	年間減価償却費	1 年後の固定資産残高	2 年後の固定資産残高	3 年後の固定資産残高	4 年後の固定資産残高
土地	85,000	永久	–	85,000	85,000	85,000	85,000
製造設備	50,000	8	6,250	43,750	37,500	31,250	25,000
事務所	40,000	20	2,000	38,000	36,000	34,000	32,000
合計	175,000		8,250	166,750	158,500	150,250	142,000

「昭和せんべい」の固定資産への投資 175,000 ドルの内訳を確認すると，土地が 85,000 ドル，生産設備が 50,000 ドル，事務所の建物が 40,000 ドルでした。そして設備の耐用年数は 8 年，事務所の耐用年数は 20 年とします。

年間の製造設備の減価償却費は 50,000 を 8 年で割った 6,250 ドル，事務所の減価償却費は 40,000 を 20 年で割った 2,000 ドルとなります。

減価償却を計上した後の固定資産の残高がその分減少していることも確認してください。なお，土地に耐用年数という概念がないことはすでにお伝えしたとおりです。

土地，設備，事務所という固定資産のうち，設備の減価償却は製造間接費にあたります。製造間接費はいったん棚卸資産に計上されます。

一方で，事務所の減価償却は製造間接費ではなく販管費です。販管費は直接PL に影響を与える期間費用です。

costs that directly hit the IS.

Activity 6 records the depreciation of Showa Senbei's machinery which is a manufacturing overhead. This Activity also includes the cost of the other manufacturing overheads.

The other manufacturing overheads include light and heat totaling $5,000. These expenses are paid on credit, so they are not paid immediately.

- The depreciation of machinery reduces the value of fixed assets (PP&E) in the BS by $6,250 (A).
- Other overheads of $5,000 are entered in accounts payables in the BS (B).
- Inventories in the BS increase by $11,250 covering the total depreciation and other manufacturing overheads (C).

Income Statement	損益計算書	After 5 活動5後	Act.6 活動6	After 6 活動6後
Sales (Revenue)	売上高（営業収益）	0		0
− Cost of Goods Sold	売上原価	0		0
= Gross Margin	売上総利益	0	0	0
− Selling, General & Administrative Expenses	販管費	0		0
= Income from Operations	営業利益	0	0	0
+/− Non-operating Profit/Expenses	営業外損益	0		0
− Income Taxes	法人所得税等	0		0
= Net Income	当期純利益	0	0	0

Cash Flow Statement	キャッシュフロー計算書	After 5 活動5後	Act.6 活動6	After 6 活動6後
Cash Receipts from Customers	売上収入	0		0
− Cash Paid to Suppliers and Employees	経費の支払いによる支出	34,500		34,500
− Income Taxes Paid	法人所得税等の支払い	0		0
=A Cash Flows from Operating Activities	営業活動によるキャッシュフロー	−34,500	0	−34,500
− Purchase of Property, Plant & Equipment	固定資産の取得	175,000		175,000
− Purchase of Marketable Securities	金融資産の取得	0		0
=B Cash Flows from Investing Activities	投資活動によるキャッシュフロー	−175,000	0	−175,000
Increase in Debt	借入金・社債の増加	200,000		200,000
− Interests Paid	利息支払い	0		0
− Dividends Paid	配当支払い	0		0
+ Issuance of Common Stock	株式の発行	100,000		100,000
=C Cash Flows from Financing Activities	財務活動によるキャッシュフロー	300,000	0	300,000
A+B+C Change in Cash	現金の増減額	90,500	0	90,500

活動 6 では製造間接費にあたる設備の減価償却と，その他の製造間接費を記録します。

その他の光熱費などの製造間接費は合計で 5,000 ドルとします。この費用はすぐに支払う必要はありません（掛けでの取引）。

● 製造設備の減価償却費 6,250 ドルを BS の固定資産から減額します（A）。

● その他の製造間接費 5,000 ドルを BS の仕入債務に計上します（B）。
● 減価償却費と製造間接費の合計分，BS の棚卸資産が 11,250 ドル増加します（C）。

	Balance Sheet	貸借対照表	After 5 活動5後	Act.6 活動6	After 6 活動6後
	Cash	現金	90,500	0	90,500
+	Marketable Securities	金融資産（有価証券）	0		0
+	Accounts Receivable	売上債権（売掛金）	0		0
+	Inventories	棚卸資産（在庫）	114,500	C 11,250	125,750
+	Prepaid Expenses	前払費用	0		0
+	Other Current Assets	その他流動資産	0		0
=	Current Assets	流動資産	205,000	11,250	216,250
+	Property, Plant & Equipment	有形固定資産	175,000	A -6,250	168,750
+	Financial Investment	金融投資	0		0
+	Other Fixed Assets	その他固定資産	0		0
=	Total Assets	資産合計	380,000	5,000	385,000
	Accounts Payable	仕入債務（買掛金）	80,000	B 5,000	85,000
+	Accrued Expenses	未払費用	0		0
+	Income Taxes Payable	未払法人所得税	0		0
+	Advanced Payment	前受金	0		0
+	Current Portion of Debt	短期社債・借入金	50,000		50,000
+	Other Current Liabilities	その他流動負債	0		0
=a	Current Liabilities	流動負債	130,000	5,000	135,000
	Long-term Debt	長期社債・借入金	150,000		150,000
+	Other Fixed Liabilities	その他固定負債	0		0
=b	Fixed Liabilities	固定負債	150,000	0	150,000
a+b=c	Total Liabilities	負債合計	280,000	5,000	285,000
	Capital Stock	資本金	100,000	0	100,000
+	Retained Earnings	利益剰余金	0		0
=d	Shareholders' Equity	株主資本合計	100,000	0	100,000
c+d	Total Liabilities & Equity	負債及び資本合計	380,000	5,000	385,000

Activity 7 records the depreciation of the office building along with the other SG&A expenses.

For other SG&A expenses, Showa Senbei spends $5,000 for advertisement (on credit) and pays your salary as CEO which includes the take-home pay of $26,250, and other associated items such as social security fee of $14,000 which the company will pay in the future.

- The office depreciation reduces the value of PP&E by $2,000 (A).
- The $5,000 advertising expense is entered in accounts payables in the BS (B).
- $26,250 take-home CEO salary is paid (C), which reduces the cash balance in the BS (D).
- The salary-related expense of $14,000 is entered in accrued expenses (E).
- The above total of $47,250 is recorded as SG&A expenses (F).
- The expense of $47,250 is linked to retained earnings in the BS (G).

Income Statement	損益計算書	After 6 活動6後	Act.7 活動7	After 7 活動7後
Sales (Revenue)	売上高 (営業収益)	0		0
− Cost of Goods Sold	売上原価	0		0
= Gross Margin	売上総利益	0	0	0
− Selling, General & Administrative Expenses	販管費	0	**F** 47,250	47,250
= Income from Operations	営業利益	0	−47,250	−47,250
+/− Non-operating Profit/Expenses	営業外損益	0		0
− Income Taxes	法人所得税等	0		0
= Net Income	当期純利益	0	−47,250	−47,250

Cash Flow Statement	キャッシュフロー計算書	After 6 活動6後	Act.7 活動7	After 7 活動7後
Cash Receipts from Customers	売上収入	0		0
− Cash Paid to Suppliers and Employees	経費の支払いによる支出	34,500	**C** 26,250	60,750
− Income Taxes Paid	法人所得税等の支払い	0		0
=A Cash Flows from Operating Activities	営業活動によるキャッシュフロー	−34,500	−26,250	−60,750
− Purchase of Property, Plant & Equipment	固定資産の取得	175,000		175,000
− Purchase of Marketable Securities	金融資産の取得	0		0
=B Cash Flows from Investing Activities	投資活動によるキャッシュフロー	−175,000	0	−175,000
Increase in Debt	借入金・社債の増加	200,000		200,000
− Interests Paid	利息支払い	0		0
− Dividends Paid	配当支払い	0		0
+ Issuance of Common Stock	株式の発行	100,000		100,000
=C Cash Flows from Financing Activities	財務活動によるキャッシュフロー	300,000	0	300,000
A+B+C Change in Cash	現金の増減額	90,500	−26,250	64,250

減価償却費と販管費を計上する

活動7では販管費にあたる事務所の減価償却と，その他の販管費を記録します。

その他の販管費として，販売促進費（掛けでの支払い）5,000ドルと，社長としてのあなたの給料を計上します。給料の手取り金額は26,250ドル，それに伴う社会保険料などの会社が後に支払うコストは14,000ドルとします。

- 事務所の減価償却費2,000ドルをBSの固定資産から減額します（A）。
- 販売促進費5,000ドル分のBSの仕入債務が増加します（B）。
- 社長の給与のうち，手取り分の26,250ドルを支払い（C），その分現金残高が減少します（D）。
- 給与関連費用14,000ドルは未払費用として計上します（E）。
- 上記の合計額47,250ドルを販管費として計上します（F）。
- 47,250ドルの費用はBSの利益剰余金にリンクします（G）。

	Balance Sheet	貸借対照表	After 6 活動6後	Act.7 活動7	After 7 活動7後
	Cash	現金	90,500	−26,250 D	64,250
+	Marketable Securities	金融資産（有価証券）	0		0
+	Accounts Receivable	売上債権（売掛金）	0		0
+	Inventories	棚卸資産（在庫）	125,750		125,750
+	Prepaid Expenses	前払費用	0		0
+	Other Current Assets	その他流動資産	0		0
=	Current Assets	流動資産	216,250	−26,250	190,000
+	Property, Plant & Equipment	有形固定資産	168,750	−2,000 A	166,750
+	Financial Investment	金融投資	0		0
+	Other Fixed Assets	その他固定資産	0		0
=	Total Assets	資産合計	385,000	−28,250	356,750
	Accounts Payable	仕入債務（買掛金）	85,000	5,000 B	90,000
+	Accrued Expenses	未払費用	0	14,000 E	14,000
+	Income Taxes Payable	未払法人所得税	0		0
+	Advanced Payment	前受金	0		0
+	Current Portion of Debt	短期社債・借入金	50,000		50,000
+	Other Current Liabilities	その他流動負債	0		0
=a	Current Liabilities	流動負債	135,000	19,000	154,000
	Long-term Debt	長期社債・借入金	150,000		150,000
+	Other Fixed Liabilities	その他固定負債	0		0
=b	Fixed Liabilities	固定負債	150,000	0	150,000
a+b=c	Total Liabilities	負債合計	285,000	19,000	304,000
	Capital Stock	資本金	100,000	0 G	100,000
+	Retained Earnings	利益剰余金	0	−47,250	−47,250
=d	Shareholders' Equity	株主資本合計	100,000	−47,250	52,750
c+d	Total Liabilities & Equity	負債及び資本合計	385,000	−28,250	356,750

Activity 7: Application Exercise 1

Now Showa Senbei is purchasing a small building near the factory as a research and development center to study the taste of senbei. Annual depreciation is assumed to be $1,100.

Construction has already been completed and paid for, so in this activity focus on the building's depreciation.

How do the financial statements change?

(Hint: R&D expenses are SG&A expenses)

Income Statement	損益計算書	7 Exercise 1 7 応用問題 1
Sales (Revenue)	売上高（営業収益）	
− Cost of Goods Sold	売上原価	
= Gross Margin	売上総利益	0
− Selling, General & Administrative Expenses	販管費	1,100
= Income from Operations	営業利益	−1,100
+/− Non-operating Profit/Expenses	営業外損益	
− Income Taxes	法人所得税等	
= Net Income	当期純利益	−1,100

Cash Flow Statement	キャッシュフロー計算書	7 Exercise 1 7 応用問題 1
Cash Receipts from Customers	売上収入	
− Cash Paid to Suppliers and Employees	経費の支払いによる支出	
− Income Taxes Paid	法人所得税等の支払い	
=A Cash Flows from Operating Activities	営業活動によるキャッシュフロー	0
− Purchase of Property, Plant & Equipment	固定資産の取得	
− Purchase of Marketable Securities	金融資産の取得	
=B Cash Flows from Investing Activities	投資活動によるキャッシュフロー	0
Increase in Debt	借入金・社債の増加	
− Interests Paid	利息支払い	
− Dividends Paid	配当支払い	
+ Issuance of Common Stock	株式の発行	
=C Cash Flows from Financing Activities	財務活動によるキャッシュフロー	0
A+B+C Change in Cash	現金の増減額	0

Depreciation related to R&D is directly accounted for as SG&A expenses in the IS.

工場の近くに別の小さなビルを購入して，せんべいの味を研究する研究開発
センターを建設するとします。減価償却費は 1,100 ドルです。

研究開発センターはすでに建設されているとして，ここでは減価償却のみを
記録して下さい。

財務三表はどのように変化しますか？

（ヒント：研究開発費は販管費です）

	Balance Sheet	貸借対照表	7 Exercise 1 7 応用問題 1
	Cash	現金	0
+	Marketable Securities	金融資産（有価証券）	
+	Accounts Receivable	売上債権（売掛金）	
+	Inventories	棚卸資産（在庫）	
+	Prepaid Expenses	前払費用	
+	Other Current Assets	その他流動資産	
=	Current Assets	流動資産	0
+	Property, Plant & Equipment	有形固定資産	−1,100
+	Financial Investment	金融投資	
+	Other Fixed Assets	その他固定資産	
=	Total Assets	資産合計	−1,100
	Accounts Payable	仕入債務（買掛金）	
+	Accrued Expenses	未払費用	
+	Income Taxes Payable	未払法人所得税	
+	Advanced Payment	前受金	
+	Current Portion of Debt	短期社債・借入金	
+	Other Current Liabilities	その他流動負債	
=a	Current Liabilities	流動負債	0
	Long-term Debt	長期社債・借入金	
+	Other Fixed Liabilities	その他固定負債	
=b	Fixed Liabilities	固定負債	0
a+b=c	Total Liabilities	負債合計	0
	Capital Stock	資本金	0
+	Retained Earnings	利益剰余金	−1,100
=d	Shareholders' Equity	株主資本合計	−1,100
c+d	Total Liabilities & Equity	負債及び資本合計	−1,100

研究開発にかかわる減価償却費は直接 PL の販管費として計上されます。

Activity 7: Application Exercise 2

In order to deal with the risk of food poisoning, Showa Senbei agrees to enter general liability insurance. The annual insurance premium is $2,400 and it was paid upfront. Suppose it is the end of the third month since you signed up for a one-year contract.

How do the financial statements change?

(Hint: The portion of the premium covering the first 3 months is recorded as SG&A expenses)

Income Statement	損益計算書	7 Exercise 2 7 応用問題 2
Sales (Revenue)	売上高（営業収益）	
− Cost of Goods Sold	売上原価	
= Gross Margin	売上総利益	0
− Selling, General & Administrative Expenses	販管費	600
= Income from Operations	営業利益	−600
+/− Non-operating Profit/Expenses	営業外損益	
− Income Taxes	法人所得税等	
= Net Income	当期純利益	−600

Cash Flow Statement	キャッシュフロー計算書	7 Exercise 2 7 応用問題 2
Cash Receipts from Customers	売上収入	
− Cash Paid to Suppliers and Employees	経費の支払いによる支出	2,400
− Income Taxes Paid	法人所得税等の支払い	
=A Cash Flows from Operating Activities	営業活動によるキャッシュフロー	−2,400
− Purchase of Property, Plant & Equipment	固定資産の取得	
− Purchase of Marketable Securities	金融資産の取得	
=B Cash Flows from Investing Activities	投資活動によるキャッシュフロー	0
Increase in Debt	借入金・社債の増加	
− Interests Paid	利息支払い	
− Dividends Paid	配当支払い	
+ Issuance of Common Stock	株式の発行	
=C Cash Flows from Financing Activities	財務活動によるキャッシュフロー	0
A+B+C Change in Cash	現金の増減額	−2,400

Only the fraction of the premium covering the first 3 months is accounted for as SG&A expenses. The company has a right that the remaining nine months will be covered by the insurance, therefore, record the prepaid 9 months of insurance in the assets section of the BS.

活動7：応用問題2

食中毒などを起こすリスクに対応するために，一般賠償責任保険に加入することにしました。年間の保険料は2,400ドルであり，一括で払いました。現在，1年契約の保険に加入してから3カ月目だとします。

財務三表はどのように変化しますか？
（ヒント：最初の3カ月をカバーする保険料の部分は販管費になります）

	Balance Sheet	貸借対照表	7 Exercise 2 7 応用問題2
	Cash	現金	−2,400
+	Marketable Securities	金融資産（有価証券）	
+	Accounts Receivable	売上債権（売掛金）	
+	Inventories	棚卸資産（在庫）	
+	Prepaid Expenses	前払費用	1,800
+	Other Current Assets	その他流動資産	
=	Current Assets	流動資産	−600
+	Property, Plant & Equipment	有形固定資産	
+	Financial Investment	金融投資	
+	Other Fixed Assets	その他固定資産	
=	Total Assets	資産合計	−600
	Accounts Payable	仕入債務（買掛金）	
+	Accrued Expenses	未払費用	
+	Income Taxes Payable	未払法人所得税	
+	Advanced Payment	前受金	
+	Current Portion of Debt	短期社債・借入金	
+	Other Current Liabilities	その他流動負債	
=a	Current Liabilities	流動負債	0
	Long-term Debt	長期社債・借入金	
+	Other Fixed Liabilities	その他固定負債	
=b	Fixed Liabilities	固定負債	0
a+b=c	Total Liabilities	負債合計	0
	Capital Stock	資本金	0
+	Retained Earnings	利益剰余金	−600
=d	Shareholders' Equity	株主資本合計	−600
c+d	Total Liabilities & Equity	負債及び資本合計	−600

1年分の保険料を支払っていますが，最初の3カ月をカバーする保険料の部分のみを販管費として計上します。残りの9カ月分は今後保険を受け取れる権利を持っていることになるので，前払費用としてBSの資産に計上します。

8 Pay for the Raw Materials

In Activity 3, Showa Senbei purchased $80,000 worth of raw materials or so, but did not pay at the time. Now it is time to pay some portion of it ($50,000).

- $50,000 is paid to suppliers and is recorded in the CFS accordingly (A).
- Cash balance in the BS decreases (B).
- Accounts payables located in the liability section of the BS decreases by the payment of $50,000 (C).

Note that paying for this raw material neither affects the value of inventory nor the IS.

Income Statement	損益計算書	After 7 活動7後	Act.8 活動8	After 8 活動8後
Sales (Revenue)	売上高（営業収益）	0		0
− Cost of Goods Sold	売上原価	0		0
= Gross Margin	売上総利益	0	0	0
− Selling, General, and Administrative Expenses	販管費	47,250		47,250
= Income from Operations	営業利益	−47,250	0	−47,250
+/− Non-operating Profit/Expenses	営業外損益	0		0
− Income Taxes	法人所得税等	0		0
= Net Income	当期純利益	−47,250	0	−47,250

Cash Flow Statement	キャッシュフロー計算書	After 7 活動7後	Act.8 活動8	After 8 活動8後
Cash Receipts from Customers	売上収入	0		0
− Cash Paid to Suppliers and Employees	経費の支払いによる支出	60,750 A 50,000		110,750
− Income Taxes Paid	法人所得税等の支払い	0		0
=A Cash Flows from Operating Activities	営業活動によるキャッシュフロー	−60,750	−50,000	−110,750
− Purchase of Property, Plant & Equipment	固定資産の取得	175,000		175,000
− Purchase of Marketable Securities	金融資産の取得	0		0
=B Cash Flows from Investing Activities	投資活動によるキャッシュフロー	−175,000	0	−175,000
Increase in Debt	借入金・社債の増加	200,000		200,000
− Interests Paid	利息支払い	0		0
− Dividends Paid	配当支払い	0		0
+ Issuance of Common Stock	株式の発行	100,000		100,000
=C Cash Flows from Financing Activities	財務活動によるキャッシュフロー	300,000	0	300,000
A+B+C Change in Cash	現金の増減額	64,250	−50,000	14,250

活動

8 材料費を支払う

活動3で，原材料や資材を合計で80,000ドル分仕入れましたが，その時点では代金は支払っていませんでした。この代金の一部（50,000ドル）をそろそろ支払う必要があります。

● CFSの経費の支払いによる支出に50,000ドルが計上されます（A）。
● BSの現金残高が減少します（B）。
● 支払いを行った分，BSの負債である仕入債務が50,000ドル減少します（C）。

材料費の支払い自体は棚卸資産の金額には影響しません。またPLにも影響を与えません。

Balance Sheet	貸借対照表	After 7 活動7後	Act.8 活動8	After 8 活動8後
Cash	現金	64,250	−50,000	14,250
+ Marketable Securities	金融資産（有価証券）	0		0
+ Accounts Receivable	売上債権（売掛金）	0	0	0
+ Inventories	棚卸資産（在庫）	125,750	0	125,750
+ Prepaid Expenses	前払費用	0		0
+ Other Current Assets	その他流動資産	0		0
= Current Assets	流動資産	190,000	−50,000	140,000
+ Property, Plant & Equipment	有形固定資産	166,750	0	166,750
+ Financial Investment	金融投資	0		0
+ Other Fixed Assets	その他固定資産	0		0
= Total Assets	資産合計	356,750	−50,000	306,750
Accounts Payable	仕入債務（買掛金）	90,000	−50,000	40,000
+ Accrued Expenses	未払費用	14,000		14,000
+ Income Taxes Payable	未払法人所得税	0		0
+ Advanced Payment	前受金	0		0
+ Current Portion of Debt	短期社債・借入金	50,000		50,000
+ Other Current Liabilities	その他流動負債	0		0
=a Current Liabilities	流動負債	154,000	−50,000	104,000
Long-term Debt	長期社債・借入金	150,000		150,000
+ Other Fixed Liabilities	その他固定負債	0		0
=b Fixed Liabilities	固定負債	150,000	0	150,000
a+b=c Total Liabilities	負債合計	304,000	−50,000	254,000
Capital Stock	資本金	100,000	0	100,000
+ Retained Earnings	利益剰余金	−47,250	0	−47,250
=d Shareholders' Equity	株主資本合計	52,750	0	52,750
c+d Total Liabilities & Equity	負債及び資本合計	356,750	−50,000	306,750

Pay the supplier an additional $5,000.

How do the financial statements change?

Income Statement	損益計算書	8 Exercise 8 応用問題
Sales (Revenue)	売上高（営業収益）	
− Cost of Goods Sold	売上原価	
= Gross Margin	売上総利益	0
− Selling, General & Administrative Expenses	販管費	
= Income from Operations	営業利益	0
+/− Non-operating Profit/Expenses	営業外損益	
− Income Taxes	法人所得税等	
= Net Income	当期純利益	0

	Cash Flow Statement	キャッシュフロー計算書	8 Exercise 8 応用問題
	Cash Receipts from Customers	売上収入	
−	Cash Paid to Suppliers and Employees	経費の支払いによる支出	5,000
−	Income Taxes Paid	法人所得税等の支払い	
=A	Cash Flows from Operating Activities	営業活動によるキャッシュフロー	−5,000
−	Purchase of Property, Plant & Equipment	固定資産の取得	
−	Purchase of Marketable Securities	金融資産の取得	
=B	Cash Flows from Investing Activities	投資活動によるキャッシュフロー	0
	Increase in Debt	借入金・社債の増加	
−	Interests Paid	利息支払い	
−	Dividends Paid	配当支払い	
+	Issuance of Common Stock	株式の発行	
=C	Cash Flows from Financing Activities	財務活動によるキャッシュフロー	0
A+B+C	Change in Cash	現金の増減額	−5,000

さらに追加で 5,000 ドルを仕入先に支払います。

財務三表はどのように変化しますか？

	Balance Sheet	貸借対照表	8 Exercise 8 応用問題
	Cash	現金	−5,000
+	Marketable Securities	金融資産（有価証券）	
+	Accounts Receivable	売上債権（売掛金）	0
+	Inventories	棚卸資産（在庫）	0
+	Prepaid Expenses	前払費用	
+	Other Current Assets	その他流動資産	
=	Current Assets	流動資産	−5,000
+	Property, Plant & Equipment	有形固定資産	0
+	Financial Investment	金融投資	
+	Other Fixed Assets	その他固定資産	
=	Total Assets	資産合計	−5,000
	Accounts Payable	仕入債務（買掛金）	−5,000
+	Accrued Expenses	未払費用	
+	Income Taxes Payable	未払法人所得税	
+	Advanced Payment	前受金	
+	Current Portion of Debt	短期社債・借入金	
+	Other Current Liabilities	その他流動負債	
=a	Current Liabilities	流動負債	−5,000
	Long-term Debt	長期社債・借入金	
+	Other Fixed Liabilities	その他固定負債	
=b	Fixed Liabilities	固定負債	0
a+b=c	Total Liabilities	負債合計	−5,000
	Capital Stock	資本金	0
+	Retained Earnings	利益剰余金	0
=d	Shareholders' Equity	株主資本合計	0
c+d	Total Liabilities & Equity	負債及び資本合計	−5,000

Activity

⑨ Ship Products

Showa Senbei succeeded in producing 62,875 packages of senbei, with an inventory value of $125,750, and a cost per package is $2.

Showa Senbei then received an order for 50,300 packages which is 80% of their inventories from various customers and shipped them with the price of $4 per package. Showa Senbei followed up immediately by sending invoices but must wait before it can receive payment (sales on credit).

- $201,200 (50,300 packages × $4) is recorded as sales in the IS (A).
- Since the customers have not yet paid, the amount is added to accounts receivables in the BS (B).
- Inventories are reduced by the value of the quantity shipped which is $100,600 (80% of $125,750 or 50,300 packages × $2) (C).
- The same amount is entered in cost of goods sold (D).
- The profit generated in the IS is linked to retained earnings in the BS (E).

Income Statement	損益計算書	After 8 活動8後	Act.9 活動9	After 9 活動9後
Sales (Revenue)	売上高（営業収益）	0	201,200	201,200
− Cost of Goods Sold	売上原価	0	100,600	100,600
= Gross Margin	売上総利益	0	100,600	100,600
− Selling, General & Administrative Expenses	販管費	47,250		47,250
= Income from Operations	営業利益	−47,250	100,600	53,350
+/− Non-operating Profit/Expenses	営業外損益	0		0
− Income Taxes	法人所得税等	0		0
= Net Income	当期純利益	−47,250	100,600	53,350

Cash Flow Statement	キャッシュフロー計算書	After 8 活動8後	Act.9 活動9	After 9 活動9後
Cash Receipts from Customers	売上収入	0		0
− Cash Paid to Suppliers and Employees	経費の支払いによる支出	110,750		110,750
− Income Taxes Paid	法人所得税等の支払い	0		0
=A Cash Flows from Operating Activities	営業活動によるキャッシュフロー	−110,750	0	−110,750
− Purchase of Property, Plant & Equipment	固定資産の取得	175,000		175,000
− Purchase of Marketable Securities	金融資産の取得	0		0
=B Cash Flows from Investing Activities	投資活動によるキャッシュフロー	−175,000	0	−175,000
Increase in Debt	借入金・社債の増加	200,000		200,000
− Interests Paid	利息支払い	0		0
− Dividends Paid	配当支払い	0		0
+ Issuance of Common Stock	株式の発行	100,000		100,000
=C Cash Flows from Financing Activities	財務活動によるキャッシュフロー	300,000	0	300,000
A+B+C Change in Cash	現金の増減額	14,250	0	14,250

活動
⑨ 製品を出荷する

「昭和せんべい」は 62,875 袋の生産に成功しました。棚卸資産の残高は 125,750 ドルなので，1 袋あたりの原価は 2 ドルということです。

そして，そのうち 80％にあたる 50,300 袋をさまざまな顧客から受注し出荷しました。売値は 1 袋あたり 4 ドルです。出荷後すぐに請求書を発送していますが，売上代金の回収まではしばらく待たなければなりません（掛け売り）。

- 売上を 201,200 ドル（50,300 袋× 4 ドル）計上します（A）。
- 支払いはまだですので，この額は BS の売上債権として計上されます（B）。
- 出荷した分の在庫 100,600 ドル（125,750 ドルの 80％，または 50,300 袋× 2 ドル）を減らします（C）。
- この額は売上原価となります（D）。
- PL で発生した分の利益は BS の利益剰余金にリンクします（E）。

	Balance Sheet	貸借対照表	After 8 活動8後	Act.9 活動9	After 9 活動9後
	Cash	現金	14,250	0	14,250
+	Marketable Securities	金融資産（有価証券）	0		0
+	Accounts Receivable	売上債権（売掛金）	0	201,200	201,200
+	Inventories	棚卸資産（在庫）	125,750	–100,600	25,150
+	Prepaid Expenses	前払費用	0		0
+	Other Current Assets	その他流動資産	0		0
=	Current Assets	流動資産	140,000	100,600	240,600
+	Property, Plant & Equipment	有形固定資産	166,750	0	166,750
+	Financial Investment	金融投資	0	0	0
+	Other Fixed Assets	その他固定資産	0	0	0
=	Total Assets	資産合計	306,750	100,600	407,350
	Accounts Payable	仕入債務（買掛金）	40,000		40,000
+	Accrued Expenses	未払費用	14,000		14,000
+	Income Taxes Payable	未払法人所得税	0		0
+	Advanced Payment	前受金	0		0
+	Current Portion of Debt	短期社債・借入金	50,000		50,000
+	Other Current Liabilities	その他流動負債	0		0
=a	Current Liabilities	流動負債	104,000	0	104,000
	Long-term Debt	長期社債・借入金	150,000		150,000
+	Other Fixed Liabilities	その他固定負債	0		0
=b	Fixed Liabilities	固定負債	150,000	0	150,000
a+b=c	Total Liabilities	負債合計	254,000	0	254,000
	Capital Stock	資本金	100,000	0	100,000
+	Retained Earnings	利益剰余金	–47,250	100,600	53,350
=d	Shareholders' Equity	株主資本合計	52,750	100,600	153,350
c+d	Total Liabilities & Equity	負債及び資本合計	306,750	100,600	407,350

Activity 9: Application Exercise

Showa Senbei received another order of 10,000 packages from new customers. This time the price per package is $3.90 because the customer is willing to pay cash at the shipment. Of course, there is no change in the cost of goods sold per package ($2 per package).

How do the financial statements change?

Income Statement	損益計算書	9 Exercise 9 応用問題
Sales (Revenue)	売上高（営業収益）	39,000
− Cost of Goods Sold	売上原価	20,000
= Gross Margin	売上総利益	19,000
− Selling, General & Administrative Expenses	販管費	
= Income from Operations	営業利益	19,000
+/− Non-operating Profit/Expenses	営業外損益	
− Income Taxes	法人所得税等	
= Net Income	当期純利益	19,000

Cash Flow Statement	キャッシュフロー計算書	9 Exercise 9 応用問題
Cash Receipts from Customers	売上収入	39,000
− Cash Paid to Suppliers and Employees	経費の支払いによる支出	
− Income Taxes Paid	法人所得税等の支払い	
=A Cash Flows from Operating Activities	営業活動によるキャッシュフロー	39,000
− Purchase of Property, Plant & Equipment	固定資産の取得	
− Purchase of Marketable Securities	金融資産の取得	
=B Cash Flows from Investing Activities	投資活動によるキャッシュフロー	0
Increase in Debt	借入金・社債の増加	
− Interests Paid	利息支払い	
− Dividends Paid	配当支払い	
+ Issuance of Common Stock	株式の発行	
=C Cash Flows from Financing Activities	財務活動によるキャッシュフロー	0
A+B+C Change in Cash	現金の増減額	39,000

活動 9 : 応用問題

さらに 10,000 袋の注文を新規顧客から受けました。この顧客は出荷と同時に現金を支払うため，価格は袋あたり 3.9 ドルに値引きしました。当然ながら，袋あたりの売上原価に変更はありません（袋あたり 2 ドル）。

財務三表はどのように変化しますか？

	Balance Sheet	貸借対照表	9 Exercise 9 応用問題
	Cash	現金	39,000
+	Marketable Securities	金融資産（有価証券）	
+	Accounts Receivable	売上債権（売掛金）	
+	Inventories	棚卸資産（在庫）	−20,000
+	Prepaid Expenses	前払費用	
+	Other Current Assets	その他流動資産	
=	Current Assets	流動資産	19,000
+	Property, Plant & Equipment	有形固定資産	0
+	Financial Investment	金融投資	
+	Other Fixed Assets	その他固定資産	
=	Total Assets	資産合計	19,000
	Accounts Payable	仕入債務（買掛金）	
+	Accrued Expenses	未払費用	
+	Income Taxes Payable	未払法人所得税	
+	Advanced Payment	前受金	
+	Current Portion of Debt	短期社債・借入金	
+	Other Current Liabilities	その他流動負債	
=a	Current Liabilities	流動負債	0
	Long-term Debt	長期社債・借入金	
+	Other Fixed Liabilities	その他固定負債	
=b	Fixed Liabilities	固定負債	0
a+b=c	Total Liabilities	負債合計	0
	Capital Stock	資本金	0
+	Retained Earnings	利益剰余金	19,000
=d	Shareholders' Equity	株主資本合計	19,000
c+d	Total Liabilities & Equity	負債及び資本合計	19,000

Activity

10 Collect Cash

Showa Senbei has received payment for 70% of the $201,200 shipped in Activity 9.

- Cash receipts from customers on the CFS is recorded as $140,840 (70% of $201,200) (A).
- The cash balance on the BS increases by the same amount (B).
- Accounts receivables on the BS decreases by the same amount (C).

Receiving cash payments does not affect the IS.

Income Statement	損益計算書	After 9 活動9後	Act.10 活動10	After 10 活動10後
Sales (Revenue)	売上高 (営業利益)	201,200		201,200
− Cost of Goods Sold	売上原価	100,600		100,600
= Gross Margin	売上総利益	100,600	0	100,600
− Selling, General & Administrative Expenses	販管費	47,250		47,250
= Income from Operations	営業利益	53,350	0	53,350
+/− Non-operating Profit/Expenses	営業外損益	0		0
− Income Taxes	法人所得税等	0		0
= Net Income	当期純利益	53,350	0	53,350

Cash Flow Statement	キャッシュフロー計算書	After 9 活動9後	Act.10 活動10	After 10 活動10後
Cash Receipts from Customers	売上収入	0	140,840	140,840
− Cash Paid to Suppliers and Employees	経費の支払いによる支出	110,750	A	110,750
− Income Taxes Paid	法人所得税等の支払い	0		0
=A Cash Flows from Operating Activities	営業活動によるキャッシュフロー	−110,750	140,840	30,090
− Purchase of Property, Plant & Equipment	固定資産の取得	175,000		175,000
− Purchase of Marketable Securities	金融資産の取得	0		0
=B Cash Flows from Investing Activities	投資活動によるキャッシュフロー	−175,000	0	−175,000
Increase in Debt	借入金・社債の増加	200,000		200,000
− Interests Paid	利息支払い	0		0
− Dividends Paid	配当支払い	0		0
+ Issuance of Common Stock	株式の発行	100,000		100,000
=C Cash Flows from Financing Activities	財務活動によるキャッシュフロー	300,000	0	300,000
A+B+C Change in Cash	現金の増減額	14,250	140,840	155,090

10 代金を回収する

活動9で出荷した製品201,200ドル分のうち70%に関して支払いを受け取りました。

- CFSの売上収入として140,840ドル（201,200ドル分の70%）を計上します（A）。
- BSの現金残高が同額増えます（B）。
- BSの売上債権が同額減少します（C）。

現金の支払いを受けたこと自体はPLには影響を与えません。

	Balance Sheet	貸借対照表	After 9 活動9 後	Act.10 活動10	After 10 活動10 後
	Cash	現金	14,250 B 140,840		155,090
+	Marketable Securities	金融資産（有価証券）	0		0
+	Accounts Receivable	売上債権（売掛金）	201,200 C -140,840		60,360
+	Inventories	棚卸資産（在庫）	25,150		25,150
+	Prepaid Expenses	前払費用	0		0
+	Other Current Assets	その他流動資産	0		0
=	Current Assets	流動資産	240,600	0	240,600
+	Property, Plant & Equipment	有形固定資産	166,750	0	166,750
+	Financial Investment	金融投資	0		0
+	Other Fixed Assets	その他固定資産	0		0
=	Total Assets	資産合計	407,350	0	407,350
	Accounts Payable	仕入債務（買掛金）	40,000	0	40,000
+	Accrued Expenses	未払費用	14,000		14,000
+	Income Taxes Payable	未払法人所得税	0		0
+	Advanced Payment	前受金	0		0
+	Current Portion of Debt	短期社債・借入金	50,000		50,000
+	Other Current Liabilities	その他流動負債	0		0
=a	Current Liabilities	流動負債	104,000	0	104,000
	Long-term Debt	長期社債・借入金	150,000		150,000
+	Other Fixed Liabilities	その他固定負債	0		0
=b	Fixed Liabilities	固定負債	150,000	0	150,000
a+b=c	Total Liabilities	負債合計	254,000	0	254,000
	Capital Stock	資本金	100,000	0	100,000
+	Retained Earnings	利益剰余金	53,350	0	53,350
=d	Shareholders' Equity	株主資本合計	153,350	0	153,350
c+d	Total Liabilities & Equity	負債及び資本合計	407,350	0	407,350

Activity 10: Application Exercise

What if Showa Senbei received payment for an additional 20% of the $201,200 from the senbei shipped in Activity 9.

How do the financial statements change?

Income Statement	損益計算書	10 Exercise 10 応用問題
Sales (Revenue)	売上高（営業収益）	
− Cost of Goods Sold	売上原価	
= Gross Margin	売上総利益	0
− Selling, General & Administrative Expenses	販管費	
= Income from Operations	営業利益	0
+/− Non-operating Profit/Expenses	営業外損益	
− Income Taxes	法人所得税等	
= Net Income	当期純利益	0

Cash Flow Statement	キャッシュフロー計算書	10 Exercise 10 応用問題
Cash Receipts from Customers	売上収入	40,240
− Cash Paid to Suppliers and Employees	経費の支払いによる支出	
− Income Taxes Paid	法人所得税等の支払い	
=A Cash Flows from Operating Activities	営業活動によるキャッシュフロー	40,240
− Purchase of Property, Plant & Equipment	固定資産の取得	
− Purchase of Marketable Securities	金融資産の取得	
=B Cash Flows from Investing Activities	投資活動によるキャッシュフロー	0
Increase in Debt	借入金・社債の増加	
− Interests Paid	利息支払い	
− Dividends Paid	配当支払い	
+ Issuance of Common Stock	株式の発行	
=C Cash Flows from Financing Activities	財務活動によるキャッシュフロー	0
A+B+C Change in Cash	現金の増減額	40,240

活動 10：応用問題

活動 9 で出荷した製品 201,200 ドル分のうちさらに 20％に関して支払いを受け取りました。

財務三表はどのように変化しますか？

	Balance Sheet	貸借対照表	10 Exercise 10 応用問題
	Cash	現金	40,240
+	Marketable Securities	金融資産（有価証券）	
+	Accounts Receivable	売上債権（売掛金）	−40,240
+	Inventories	棚卸資産（在庫）	
+	Prepaid Expenses	前払費用	
+	Other Current Assets	その他流動資産	
=	Current Assets	流動資産	0
+	Property, Plant & Equipment	有形固定資産	0
+	Financial Investment	金融投資	
+	Other Fixed Assets	その他固定資産	
=	Total Assets	資産合計	0
	Accounts Payable	仕入債務（買掛金）	0
+	Accrued Expenses	未払費用	
+	Income Taxes Payable	未払法人所得税	
+	Advanced Payment	前受金	
+	Current Portion of Debt	短期社債・借入金	
+	Other Current Liabilities	その他流動負債	
=a	Current Liabilities	流動負債	0
	Long-term Debt	長期社債・借入金	
+	Other Fixed Liabilities	その他固定負債	
=b	Fixed Liabilities	固定負債	0
a+b=c	Total Liabilities	負債合計	0
	Capital Stock	資本金	0
+	Retained Earnings	利益剰余金	0
=d	Shareholders' Equity	株主資本合計	0
c+d	Total Liabilities & Equity	負債及び資本合計	0

Activity 9, 10: Application Exercise

A. Suppose that Showa Senbei received an order for 10,000 packages from another customer. The price per package is agreed to be $3.80 because the customer paid $38,000 (10,000 packages×$3.80) in advance prior to shipping. Note the senbei has not shipped.

B. You shipped 10,000 packages ordered in A. Note that the cost of goods sold per package remains unchanged ($2 per package).

How do the financial statements change in A and B, respectively?

Challenging question! Think how you should deal with it.

Income Statement	損益計算書	9,10 Exercise A 9,10 応用問題 A	9,10 Exercise B 9,10 応用問題 B
Sales (Revenue)	売上高（営業収益）		38,000
− Cost of Goods Sold	売上原価		20,000
= Gross Margin	売上総利益	0	18,000
− Selling, General & Administrative Expenses	販管費		
= Income from Operations	営業利益	0	18,000
+/− Non-operating Profit/Expenses	営業外損益		
− Income Taxes	法人所得税等		
= Net Income	当期純利益	0	18,000

Cash Flow Statement	キャッシュフロー計算書	9,10 Exercise A 9,10 応用問題 A	9,10 Exercise B 9,10 応用問題 B
Cash Receipts from Customers	売上収入	38,000	
− Cash Paid to Suppliers and Employees	経費の支払いによる支出		
− Income Taxes Paid	法人所得税等の支払い		
=A Cash Flows from Operating Activities	営業活動によるキャッシュフロー	38,000	0
− Purchase of Property, Plant & Equipment	固定資産の取得		
− Purchase of Marketable Securities	金融資産の取得		
=B Cash Flows from Investing Activities	投資活動によるキャッシュフロー	0	0
Increase in Debt	借入金・社債の増加		
− Interests Paid	利息支払い		
− Dividends Paid	配当支払い		
+ Issuance of Common Stock	株式の発行		
=C Cash Flows from Financing Activities	財務活動によるキャッシュフロー	0	0
A+B+C Change in Cash	現金の増減額	38,000	0

Sales are recorded at the time of shipment, so if you received the payment earlier, it is treated as a liability on the BS as an advanced payment. It is a liability because the advance payment makes the company obligated to ship the ordered quantity of senbei.

A. 別の顧客から 10,000 袋の注文を受けました。1 袋あたりの価格は 3.8 ド
ルですが，顧客は，出荷に先立って代金 38,000 ドル（10,000 袋× 3.8 ドル）
を振り込んできました。まだ製品は出荷していません。

B. A で注文された 10,000 袋を出荷しました。なお，袋あたりの売上原価
に変更はありません（袋あたり 2 ドル）。

A，B それぞれで，財務三表はどのように変化しますか？

ちょっと難問です。どう扱うか考えてみてください。

Balance Sheet	貸借対照表	9,10 Exercise A 9,10 応用問題 A	9,10 Exercise B 9,10 応用問題 B
Cash	現金	38,000	0
+ Marketable Securities	金融資産（有価証券）		
+ Accounts Receivable	売上債権（売掛金）		
+ Inventories	棚卸資産（在庫）		−20,000
+ Prepaid Expenses	前払費用		
+ Other Current Assets	その他流動資産		
= Current Assets	流動資産	38,000	−20,000
+ Property, Plant & Equipment	有形固定資産	0	0
+ Financial Investment	金融投資		
+ Other Fixed Assets	その他固定資産		
= Total Assets	資産合計	38,000	−20,000
Accounts Payable	仕入債務（買掛金）	0	
+ Accrued Expenses	未払費用		
+ Income Taxes Payable	未払法人所得税		
+ Advanced Payment	前受金	38,000	−38,000
+ Current Portion of Debt	短期社債・借入金		
+ Other Current Liabilities	その他流動負債		
=a Current Liabilities	流動負債	38,000	−38,000
Long-term Debt	長期社債・借入金		
+ Other Fixed Liabilities	その他固定負債		
=b Fixed Liabilities	固定負債	0	0
a+b=c Total Liabilities	負債合計	38,000	−38,000
Capital Stock	資本金	0	0
+ Retained Earnings	利益剰余金	0	18,000
=d Shareholders' Equity	株主資本合計	0	18,000
c+d Total Liabilities & Equity	負債及び資本合計	38,000	−20,000

売上の計上は出荷する時点で行いますので，それ以前に代金を受け取った場
合は BS の負債である前受金として処理します。注文された分を，その後に出
荷する義務を負っているので債務なのです。

Activity

11 Write-off Cost

Unfortunately, one of the customers who we shipped 2,000 packages to during Activity 9 went bankrupt. This means Showa Senbei can no longer collect money for the 2,000 packages and has to reduce accounts receivables and record losses.

● The loss of $8,000 (2,000 packages × $4) is recorded as a bad debt expense as a SG&A expense on the IS (A).

● This $8,000 reduces accounts receivables on the BS because it is no longer recoverable (B).

● The loss in the IS reduces retained earnings in the BS (C).

	Income Statement	損益計算書	After 10 活動10後	Act.11 活動11	After 11 活動11後
	Sales (Revenue)	売上高（営業収益）	201,200		201,200
−	Cost of Goods Sold	売上原価	100,600		100,600
=	Gross Margin	売上総利益	100,600	0	100,600
−	Selling, General & Administrative Expenses	販管費	47,250 A	8,000	55,250
=	Income from Operations	営業利益	53,350	−8,000	45,350
+/−	Non-operating Profit/Expenses	営業外損益	0		0
−	Income Taxes	法人所得税等	0		0
=	Net Income	当期純利益	53,350	−8,000	45,350

	Cash Flow Statement	キャッシュフロー計算書	After 10 活動10後	Act.11 活動11	After 11 活動11後
	Cash Receipts from Customers	売上収入	140,840	0	140,840
−	Cash Paid to Suppliers and Employees	経費の支払いによる支出	110,750		110,750
−	Income Taxes Paid	法人所得税等の支払い	0		0
=A	Cash Flows from Operating Activities	営業活動によるキャッシュフロー	30,090	0	30,090
−	Purchase of Property, Plant & Equipment	固定資産の取得	175,000		175,000
−	Purchase of Marketable Securities	金融資産の取得	0		0
=B	Cash Flows from Investing Activities	投資活動によるキャッシュフロー	−175,000	0	−175,000
	Increase in Debt	借入金・社債の増加	200,000		200,000
−	Interests Paid	利息支払い	0		0
−	Dividends Paid	配当支払い	0		0
+	Issuance of Common Stock	株式の発行	100,000		100,000
=C	Cash Flows from Financing Activities	財務活動によるキャッシュフロー	300,000	0	300,000
A+B+C	Change in Cash	現金の増減額	155,090	0	155,090

11 貸倒れが発生する

残念なことに，活動9で出荷した顧客のうち，2,000袋分を出荷した顧客が倒産しました。この分の代金を回収できなくなってしまったので，売上債権を減らし，損失を計上しなくてはなりません。

● PLの販管費で8,000ドル（2,000袋 × 4ドル）の貸倒れ損失を計上します（A）。

● この8,000ドルは回収が不可能となったためBSの売上債権を減少させます（B）。

● PLの損失分はBSの利益剰余金を減少させます（C）。

	Balance Sheet	貸借対照表	After 10 活動10後	Act.11 活動11	After 11 活動11後
	Cash	現金	155,090	0	155,090
+	Marketable Securities	金融資産（有価証券）	0	**B**	0
+	Accounts Receivable	売上債権（売掛金）	60,360	−8,000	52,360
+	Inventories	棚卸資産（在庫）	25,150		25,150
+	Prepaid Expenses	前払費用	0		0
+	Other Current Assets	その他流動資産	0		0
=	Current Assets	流動資産	240,600	−8,000	232,600
+	Property, Plant & Equipment	有形固定資産	166,750	0	166,750
+	Financial Investment	金融投資	0		0
+	Other Fixed Assets	その他固定資産	0		0
=	Total Assets	資産合計	407,350	−8,000	399,350
	Accounts Payable	仕入債務（買掛金）	40,000	0	40,000
+	Accrued Expenses	未払費用	14,000		14,000
+	Income Taxes Payable	未払法人所得税	0		0
+	Advanced Payment	前受金	0		0
+	Current Portion of Debt	短期社債・借入金	50,000		50,000
+	Other Current Liabilities	その他流動負債	0		0
=a	Current Liabilities	流動負債	104,000	0	104,000
	Long-term Debt	長期社債・借入金	150,000		150,000
+	Other Fixed Liabilities	その他固定負債	0		0
=b	Fixed Liabilities	固定負債	150,000	0	150,000
a+b=c	Total Liabilities	負債合計	254,000	0	254,000
	Capital Stock	資本金	100,000	0	100,000
+	Retained Earnings	利益剰余金	53,350	**C** −8,000	45,350
=d	Shareholders' Equity	株主資本合計	153,350	−8,000	145,350
c+d	Total Liabilities & Equity	負債及び資本合計	407,350	−8,000	399,350

Suppose the payment for the 10,000 packages sold at $4.20 per package is judged to be uncollectible. Record this as a loss.

How do the financial statements change?

Income Statement	損益計算書	11 Exercise 11 応用問題
Sales (Revenue)	売上高（営業収益）	
− Cost of Goods Sold	売上原価	
= Gross Margin	売上総利益	0
− Selling, General & Administrative Expenses	販管費	42,000
= Income from Operations	営業利益	−42,000
+/− Non-operating Profit/Expenses	営業外損益	
− Income Taxes	法人所得税等	
= Net Income	当期純利益	−42,000

Cash Flow Statement	キャッシュフロー計算書	11 Exercise 11 応用問題
Cash Receipts from Customers	売上収入	0
− Cash Paid to Suppliers and Employees	経費の支払いによる支出	
− Income Taxes Paid	法人所得税等の支払い	
=A Cash Flows from Operating Activities	営業活動によるキャッシュフロー	0
− Purchase of Property, Plant & Equipment	固定資産の取得	
− Purchase of Marketable Securities	金融資産の取得	
=B Cash Flows from Investing Activities	投資活動によるキャッシュフロー	0
Increase in Debt	借入金・社債の増加	
− Interests Paid	利息支払い	
− Dividends Paid	配当支払い	
+ Issuance of Common Stock	株式の発行	
=C Cash Flows from Financing Activities	財務活動によるキャッシュフロー	0
A+B+C Change in Cash	現金の増減額	0

仮に 1 袋あたり 4.2 ドルで販売した 10,000 袋分の代金回収が不可能になった
とします。損失を計上してください。

財務三表はどのように変化しますか？

	Balance Sheet	貸借対照表	11 Exercise 11 応用問題
	Cash	現金	0
+	Marketable Securities	金融資産（有価証券）	
+	Accounts Receivable	売上債権（売掛金）	−42,000
+	Inventories	棚卸資産（在庫）	
+	Prepaid Expenses	前払費用	
+	Other Current Assets	その他流動資産	
=	Current Assets	流動資産	−42,000
+	Property, Plant & Equipment	有形固定資産	0
+	Financial Investment	金融投資	
+	Other Fixed Assets	その他固定資産	
=	Total Assets	資産合計	−42,000
	Accounts Payable	仕入債務（買掛金）	0
+	Accrued Expenses	未払費用	
+	Income Taxes Payable	未払法人所得税	
+	Advanced Payment	前受金	
+	Current Portion of Debt	短期社債・借入金	
+	Other Current Liabilities	その他流動負債	
=a	Current Liabilities	流動負債	0
	Long-term Debt	長期社債・借入金	
+	Other Fixed Liabilities	その他固定負債	
=b	Fixed Liabilities	固定負債	0
a+b=c	Total Liabilities	負債合計	0
	Capital Stock	資本金	0
+	Retained Earnings	利益剰余金	−42,000
=d	Shareholders' Equity	株主資本合計	−42,000
c+d	Total Liabilities & Equity	負債及び資本合計	−42,000

In Activity 1, Showa Senbei borrowed $200,000 at a 5% interest rate. Now the interest payment is due. Keep in mind, paying interest is a non-operating expense.

- Interest of $10,000 (5% of $200,000) is paid, changing the CFS (A).
- The cash balance on the BS decreases by $10,000 (B).
- Record as a negative $10,000 (because it is an expense) for non-operating profit/expenses in the IS (C).
- The loss recorded in the IS reduces retained earnings in the BS (D).

Income Statement	損益計算書	After 11 活動11後	Act.12 活動12	After 12 活動12後
Sales (Revenue)	売上高 (営業収益)	201,200		201,200
− Cost of Goods Sold	売上原価	100,600		100,600
= Gross Margin	売上総利益	100,600	0	100,600
− Selling, General & Administrative Expenses	販管費	55,250		55,250
= Income from Operations	営業利益	45,350	0	45,350
+/− Non-operating Profit/Expenses	営業外損益	0	−10,000 C	−10,000
− Income Taxes	法人所得税等	0		0
= Net Income	当期純利益	45,350	−10,000	35,350

Cash Flow Statement	キャッシュフロー計算書	After 11 活動11後	Act.12 活動12	After 12 活動12後
Cash Receipts from Customers	売上収入	140,840		140,840
− Cash Paid to Suppliers and Employees	経費の支払いによる支出	110,750		110,750
− Income Taxes Paid	法人所得税等の支払い	0		0
=A Cash Flows from Operating Activities	営業活動によるキャッシュフロー	30,090	0	30,090
− Purchase of Property, Plant & Equipment	固定資産の取得	175,000		175,000
− Purchase of Marketable Securities	金融資産の取得	0		0
=B Cash Flows from Investing Activities	投資活動によるキャッシュフロー	−175,000	0	−175,000
Increase in Debt	借入金・社債の増加	200,000		200,000
− Interests Paid	利息支払い	0	10,000 A	10,000
− Dividends Paid	配当支払い	0		0
+ Issuance of Common Stock	株式の発行	100,000		100,000
=C Cash Flows from Financing Activities	財務活動によるキャッシュフロー	300,000	−10,000	290,000
A+B+C Change in Cash	現金の増減額	155,090	−10,000	145,090

12 利息を支払う

活動1では200,000ドルを5%の金利で借り入れました。利息を支払いましょう。利息の支払いは営業外費用です。

● 利息支払い分 10,000 ドル（200,000 ドルの 5%）を CFS に記録します（A）。
● BS の現金残高が 10,000 ドル減少します（B）。
● PL の営業外損益で 10,000 ドルのマイナスを計上します（費用なのでマイナス）（C）。
● PL の損失分 BS の利益剰余金が減少します（D）。

	Balance Sheet	貸借対照表	After 11 活動11後	Act.12 活動12	After 12 活動12後
	Cash	現金	155,090	−10,000 B	145,090
+	Marketable Securities	金融資産（有価証券）	0		0
+	Accounts Receivable	売上債権（売掛金）	52,360		52,360
+	Inventories	棚卸資産（在庫）	25,150		25,150
+	Prepaid Expenses	前払費用	0		0
+	Other Current Assets	その他流動資産	0		0
=	Current Assets	流動資産	232,600	−10,000	222,600
+	Property, Plant & Equipment	有形固定資産	166,750	0	166,750
+	Financial Investment	金融投資	0		0
+	Other Fixed Assets	その他固定資産	0		0
=	Total Assets	資産合計	399,350	−10,000	389,350
	Accounts Payable	仕入債務（買掛金）	40,000	0	40,000
+	Accrued Expenses	未払費用	14,000		14,000
+	Income Taxes Payable	未払法人所得税	0		0
+	Advanced Payment	前受金	0		0
+	Current Portion of Debt	短期社債・借入金	50,000		50,000
+	Other Current Liabilities	その他流動負債	0		0
=a	Current Liabilities	流動負債	104,000	0	104,000
	Long−term Debt	長期社債・借入金	150,000		150,000
+	Other Fixed Liabilities	その他固定負債	0		0
=b	Fixed Liabilities	固定負債	150,000	0	150,000
a+b=c	Total Liabilities	負債合計	254,000	0	254,000
	Capital Stock	資本金	100,000 D	0	100,000
+	Retained Earnings	利益剰余金	45,350	−10,000	35,350
=d	Shareholders' Equity	株主資本合計	145,350	−10,000	135,350
c+d	Total Liabilities & Equity	負債及び資本合計	399,350	−10,000	389,350

13 Repay Debt (Pay Principal)

In addition to the interest, as we saw in Activity 12, we must also pay back the $50,000 principal from the $200,000 borrowed in Activity 1 (The principal payment of $200,000 was supposed to be paid over 4 years).

● The debt repayment of $50,000 negatively affects the CFS, which decreases the company's debt (the opposite of "increase in Debt in the CFS") (A).
● The cash balance on the BS decreases by $50,000 (B).
● Long-term debt on the BS decreases by $50,000 (C).

Although $50,000 is repaid from the current portion of debt, the next payment of $50,000 moves from long-term debt and becomes a current portion of debt. Therefore, the balance of the current portion of debt does not change, while the long-term debt on the BS is reduced by $50,000.

Income Statement	損益計算書	After 12 活動12後	Act.13 活動13	After 13 活動13後
Sales (Revenue)	売上高 (営業収益)	201,200		201,200
− Cost of Goods Sold	売上原価	100,600		100,600
= Gross Margin	売上総利益	100,600	0	100,600
− Selling, General & Administrative Expenses	販管費	55,250		55,250
= Income from Operations	営業利益	45,350	0	45,350
+/− Non-operating Profit/Expenses	営業外損益	−10,000		−10,000
− Income Taxes	法人所得税等	0		0
= Net Income	当期純利益	35,350	0	35,350

Cash Flow Statement	キャッシュフロー計算書	After 12 活動12後	Act.13 活動13	After 13 活動13後
Cash Receipts from Customers	売上収入	140,840		140,840
− Cash Paid to Suppliers and Employees	経費の支払いによる支出	110,750	0	110,750
− Income Taxes Paid	法人所得税等の支払い	0		0
=A Cash Flows from Operating Activities	営業活動によるキャッシュフロー	30,090	0	30,090
− Purchase of Property, Plant & Equipment	固定資産の取得	175,000		175,000
− Purchase of Marketable Securities	金融資産の取得	0		0
=B Cash Flows from Investing Activities	投資活動によるキャッシュフロー	−175,000	0	−175,000
Increase in Debt	借入金・社債の増加	200,000	−50,000	150,000
− Interests Paid	利息支払い	10,000 A		10,000
− Dividends Paid	配当支払い	0		0
+ Issuance of Common Stock	株式の発行	100,000		100,000
=C Cash Flows from Financing Activities	財務活動によるキャッシュフロー	290,000	−50,000	240,000
A+B+C Change in Cash	現金の増減額	145,090	−50,000	95,090

活動 12 で記録した利息支払いに加えて，活動 1 で借り入れた 200,000 ドル
のうち，50,000 ドル分を返済しなければなりません（借り入れた 200,000 ドルは，
毎年 50,000 ドルずつ 4 年間で元本返済することになっていました）。

● CFS の借入金・社債の増加の項目で 50,000 ドルをマイナスします（減少して
  いるため）（A）。
● BS の現金残高が 50,000 ドル減少します（B）。
● BS の長期社債・借入金を 50,000 ドル減らします（C）。

なお，50,000 ドル分は短期社債・借入金に計上されていたものが返済された
のですが，次に支払われる 50,000 ドルが長期から短期に移るため，短期社債・
借入金の残高は変化せず，BS の長期社債・借入金が 50,000 ドル減ることにな
ります。

	Balance Sheet	貸借対照表	After 12 活動12後	Act.13 活動13	After 13 活動13後
	Cash	現金	145,090	−50,000	95,090
+	Marketable Securities	金融資産（有価証券）	0	B	0
+	Accounts Receivable	売上債権（売掛金）	52,360		52,360
+	Inventories	棚卸資産（在庫）	25,150		25,150
+	Prepaid Expenses	前払費用	0		0
+	Other Current Assets	その他流動資産	0		0
=	Current Assets	流動資産	222,600	−50,000	172,600
+	Property, Plant & Equipment	有形固定資産	166,750		166,750
+	Financial Investment	金融投資	0		0
+	Other Fixed Assets	その他固定資産	0		0
=	Total Assets	資産合計	389,350	−50,000	339,350
	Accounts Payable	仕入債務（買掛金）	40,000	0	40,000
+	Accrued Expenses	未払費用	14,000		14,000
+	Income Taxes Payable	未払法人所得税	0		0
+	Advanced Payment	前受金	0		0
+	Current Portion of Debt	短期社債・借入金	50,000		50,000
+	Other Current Liabilities	その他流動負債	0		0
=a	Current Liabilities	流動負債	104,000	0	104,000
	Long-term Debt	長期社債・借入金	150,000	−50,000	100,000
+	Other Fixed Liabilities	その他固定負債	0	C	0
=b	Fixed Liabilities	固定負債	150,000	−50,000	100,000
a+b=c	Total Liabilities	負債合計	254,000	−50,000	204,000
	Capital Stock	資本金	100,000	0	100,000
+	Retained Earnings	利益剰余金	35,350	0	35,350
=d	Shareholders' Equity	株主資本合計	135,350	0	135,350
c+d	Total Liabilities & Equity	負債及び資本合計	389,350	−50,000	339,350

14 Clear Inventory

The end of the fiscal year is approaching, and there are still 12,575 packages of senbei left in the warehouse (that corresponds to 62,875 packages produced minus 50,300 packages sold in Activity 9). Unfortunately, 2,000 packages of them have expired and must be disposed of. Showa Senbei decided to sell the remaining 10,575 with a special discount price of $2.50 per package (on credit).

- $26,438 (10,575 packages × $2.50) is recorded as sales in the IS (A).
- Since the customers have not yet paid, the amount is added to accounts receivables in the BS (B).
- Inventories are reduced by $25,150 (the total of 10,575 packages sold and 2,000 packages disposed of, 12,575 packages × $2) (C).
- The same amount is entered as the cost of goods sold (D).
- Changes in profit are linked to retained earnings in the BS (E).

Income Statement	損益計算書	After 13 活動13後	Act.14 活動14	After 14 活動14後
Sales (Revenue)	売上高（営業収益）	201,200 A	26,438	227,638
− Cost of Goods Sold	売上原価	100,600 D	25,150	125,750
= Gross Margin	売上総利益	100,600	1,288	101,888
− Selling, General & Administrative Expenses	販管費	55,250		55,250
= Income from Operations	営業利益	45,350	1,288	46,638
+/− Non-operating Profit/Expenses	営業外損益	−10,000		−10,000
− Income Taxes	法人所得税等	0		0
= Net Income	当期純利益	35,350	1,288	36,638

Cash Flow Statement	キャッシュフロー計算書	After 13 活動13後	Act.14 活動14	After 14 活動14後
Cash Receipts from Customers	売上収入	140,840		140,840
− Cash Paid to Suppliers and Employees	経費の支払いによる支出	110,750	0	110,750
− Income Taxes Paid	法人所得税等の支払い	0		0
=A Cash Flows from Operating Activities	営業活動によるキャッシュフロー	30,090	0	30,090
− Purchase of Property, Plant & Equipment	固定資産の取得	175,000		175,000
− Purchase of Marketable Securities	金融資産の取得	0		0
=B Cash Flows from Investing Activities	投資活動によるキャッシュフロー	−175,000	0	−175,000
Increase in Debt	借入金・社債の増加	150,000		150,000
− Interests Paid	利息支払い	10,000		10,000
− Dividends Paid	配当支払い	0		0
+ Issuance of Common Stock	株式の発行	100,000		100,000
=C Cash Flows from Financing Activities	財務活動によるキャッシュフロー	240,000	0	240,000
A+B+C Change in Cash	現金の増減額	95,090	0	95,090

14 在庫を整理する

　会計年度の終わりが近づいてきました。倉庫にはまだ 12,575 袋せんべいの在庫が残っています（生産した 62,875 袋から活動 9 で販売した 50,300 袋を差し引いた残り）。残念ながら，そのうち 2,000 袋は消費期限が切れていますので廃棄しなければなりません。残りの 10,575 袋に関しては 2.5 ドルに特別値引きをした上で販売することにしました（掛け売り）。

● PL に売上として 26,438 ドル（10,575 袋× 2.5 ドル）を計上します（A）。
● 掛け売りですので同額を売上債権が増加します（B）。

● BS の棚卸資産を 25,150 ドル減少させます（10,575 袋分の売上原価と，廃棄した 2,000 袋分の損失の合計，12,575 袋× 2 ドル）（C）。
● 同額を PL の売上原価に計上します（D）。
● 利益の変化分は BS の利益剰余金にリンクします（E）。

	Balance Sheet	貸借対照表	After 13 活動13後	Act.14 活動14	After 14 活動14後
	Cash	現金	95,090	0	95,090
+	Marketable Securities	金融資産（有価証券）	0		0
+	Accounts Receivable	売上債権（売掛金）	52,360 [B]	26,438	78,798
+	Inventories	棚卸資産（在庫）	25,150	−25,150	0
+	Prepaid Expenses	前払費用	0 [C]		0
+	Other Current Assets	その他流動資産	0		0
=	Current Assets	流動資産	172,600	1,288	173,888
+	Property, Plant & Equipment	有形固定資産	166,750		166,750
+	Financial Investment	金融投資	0		0
+	Other Fixed Assets	その他固定資産	0		0
=	Total Assets	資産合計	339,350	1,288	340,638
	Accounts Payable	仕入債務（買掛金）	40,000		40,000
+	Accrued Expenses	未払費用	14,000		14,000
+	Income Taxes Payable	未払法人所得税	0		0
+	Advanced Payment	前受金	0		0
+	Current Portion of Debt	短期社債・借入金	50,000		50,000
+	Other Current Liabilities	その他流動負債	0		0
=a	Current Liabilities	流動負債	104,000	0	104,000
	Long−term Debt	長期社債・借入金	100,000		100,000
+	Other Fixed Liabilities	その他固定負債	0		0
=b	Fixed Liabilities	固定負債	100,000	0	100,000
a+b=c	Total Liabilities	負債合計	204,000	0	204,000
	Capital Stock	資本金	100,000		100,000
+	Retained Earnings	利益剰余金	35,350 [E]	1,288	36,638
=d	Shareholders' Equity	株主資本合計	135,350	1,288	136,638
c+d	Total Liabilities & Equity	負債及び資本合計	339,350	1,288	340,638

Activity 14: Application Exercise

3,000 packages of senbei in the warehouse have expired. Dispose of them and record the loss. The cost is $2 per package.

How do the financial statements change?

Income Statement	損益計算書	14 Exercise 14 応用問題
Sales (Revenue)	売上高（営業収益）	
− Cost of Goods Sold	売上原価	6,000
= Gross Margin	売上総利益	−6,000
− Selling, General & Administrative Expenses	販管費	
= Income from Operations	営業利益	−6,000
+/− Non-operating Profit/Expenses	営業外損益	
− Income Taxes	法人所得税等	
= Net Income	当期純利益	−6,000

Cash Flow Statement	キャッシュフロー計算書	14 Exercise 14 応用問題
Cash Receipts from Customers	売上収入	
− Cash Paid to Suppliers and Employees	経費の支払いによる支出	0
− Income Taxes Paid	法人所得税等の支払い	
=A Cash Flows from Operating Activities	営業活動によるキャッシュフロー	0
− Purchase of Property, Plant & Equipment	固定資産の取得	
− Purchase of Marketable Securities	金融資産の取得	
=B Cash Flows from Investing Activities	投資活動によるキャッシュフロー	0
Increase in Debt	借入金・社債の増加	
− Interests Paid	利息支払い	
− Dividends Paid	配当支払い	
+ Issuance of Common Stock	株式の発行	
=C Cash Flows from Financing Activities	財務活動によるキャッシュフロー	0
A+B+C Change in Cash	現金の増減額	0

倉庫内のせんべい 3,000 袋が消費期限切れになっているとします。廃棄して損失を計上する処理をしなければなりません。なお原価は袋あたり 2 ドルです。損失を計上してください。

財務三表はどのように変化しますか？

	Balance Sheet	貸借対照表	14 Exercise 14 応用問題
	Cash	現金	0
+	Marketable Securities	金融資産（有価証券）	
+	Accounts Receivable	売上債権（売掛金）	
+	Inventories	棚卸資産（在庫）	−6,000
+	Prepaid Expenses	前払費用	
+	Other Current Assets	その他流動資産	
=	Current Assets	流動資産	−6,000
+	Property, Plant & Equipment	有形固定資産	
+	Financial Investment	金融投資	
+	Other Fixed Assets	その他固定資産	
=	Total Assets	資産合計	−6,000
	Accounts Payable	仕入債務（買掛金）	
+	Accrued Expenses	未払費用	
+	Income Taxes Payable	未払法人所得税	
+	Advanced Payment	前受金	
+	Current Portion of Debt	短期社債・借入金	
+	Other Current Liabilities	その他流動負債	
=a	Current Liabilities	流動負債	0
	Long-term Debt	長期社債・借入金	
+	Other Fixed Liabilities	その他固定負債	
=b	Fixed Liabilities	固定負債	0
a+b=c	Total Liabilities	負債合計	0
	Capital Stock	資本金	
+	Retained Earnings	利益剰余金	−6,000
=d	Shareholders' Equity	株主資本合計	−6,000
c+d	Total Liabilities & Equity	負債及び資本合計	−6,000

15 Book Income Tax

Showa Senbei is earning a profit of $36,638, which is subject to corporate income tax. Showa Senbei owes a 30% income tax bill which is actually paid a few months later.

- $10,991 (30% of $36,638 profit) is booked under income taxes in the IS (A).
- The BS is reduced by the same amount as retained earnings (B).
- At this stage, taxes are not paid, so the $10,991 worth of income taxes payable is recorded in the BS (C).

Income Statement	損益計算書	After 14 活動14後	Act.15 活動15	After 15 活動15後
Sales (Revenue)	売上高 (営業収益)	227,638		227,638
− Cost of Goods Sold	売上原価	125,750		125,750
= Gross Margin	売上総利益	101,888	0	101,888
− Selling, General & Administrative Expenses	販管費	55,250		55,250
= Income from Operations	営業利益	46,638	0	46,638
+/− Non-operating Profit/Expenses	営業外損益	−10,000		−10,000
− Income Taxes	法人所得税等	0	A 10,991	10,991
= Net Income	当期純利益	36,638	−10,991	25,646

Cash Flow Statement	キャッシュフロー計算書	After 14 活動14後	Act.15 活動15	After 15 活動15後
Cash Receipts from Customers	売上収入	140,840		140,840
− Cash Paid to Suppliers and Employees	経費の支払いによる支出	110,750		110,750
− Income Taxes Paid	法人所得税等の支払い	0		0
=A Cash Flows from Operating Activities	営業活動によるキャッシュフロー	30,090	0	30,090
− Purchase of Property, Plant & Equipment	固定資産の取得	175,000		175,000
− Purchase of Marketable Securities	金融資産の取得	0		0
=B Cash Flows from Investing Activities	投資活動によるキャッシュフロー	−175,000	0	−175,000
Increase in Debt	借入金・社債の増加	150,000		150,000
− Interests Paid	利息支払い	10,000		10,000
− Dividends Paid	配当支払い	0		0
+ Issuance of Common Stock	株式の発行	100,000		100,000
=C Cash Flows from Financing Activities	財務活動によるキャッシュフロー	240,000	0	240,000
A+B+C Change in Cash	現金の増減額	95,090	0	95,090

15 税金を計上する

ここまでで 36,638 ドルの利益を稼ぎ出している「昭和せんべい」には法人所得税が課せられます。税率は 30%です。実際に税金を支払うのは数カ月後です。

● PL で 10,991 ドル（36,638 ドルの 30%）の法人所得税を計上します（A）。
● BS で同額利益剰余金が減少します（B）。
● この段階では税金は納付してはいませんので，BS の負債で未払法人所得税が増加します（C）。

	Balance Sheet	貸借対照表	After 14 活動14後	Act.15 活動15	After 15 活動15後
	Cash	現金	95,090	0	95,090
+	Marketable Securities	金融資産（有価証券）	0		0
+	Accounts Receivable	売上債権（売掛金）	78,798		78,798
+	Inventories	棚卸資産（在庫）	0		0
+	Prepaid Expenses	前払費用	0		0
+	Other Current Assets	その他流動資産	0		0
=	Current Assets	流動資産	173,888	0	173,888
+	Property, Plant & Equipment	有形固定資産	166,750		166,750
+	Financial Investment	金融投資	0		0
+	Other Fixed Assets	その他固定資産	0		0
=	Total Assets	資産合計	340,638	0	340,638
	Accounts Payable	仕入債務（買掛金）	40,000	0	40,000
+	Accrued Expenses	未払費用	14,000		14,000
+	Income Taxes Payable	未払法人所得税	0	10,991	10,991
+	Advanced Payment	前受金	0		0
+	Current Portion of Debt	短期社債・借入金	50,000	0	50,000
+	Other Current Liabilities	その他流動負債	0		0
=a	Current Liabilities	流動負債	104,000	10,991	114,991
	Long–term Debt	長期社債・借入金	100,000		100,000
+	Other Fixed Liabilities	その他固定負債	0		0
=b	Fixed Liabilities	固定負債	100,000	0	100,000
a+b=c	Total Liabilities	負債合計	204,000	10,991	214,991
	Capital Stock	資本金	100,000	0	100,000
+	Retained Earnings	利益剰余金	36,638	–10,991	25,646
=d	Shareholders' Equity	株主資本合計	136,638	–10,991	125,646
c+d	Total Liabilities & Equity	負債及び資本合計	340,638	0	340,638

Activity

16 Declare Dividend and Pay

According to the profit generated, the board of directors of Showa Senbei (actually you) decided to pay a dividend of $0.10 per share to the shareholder (actually you). Since Showa Senbei issued 100,000 shares, the total dividend paid is $10,000.

- $10,000 is recorded under dividends paid in the CFS (A).
- The cash balance in the BS decreases by the same amount (B).
- Dividend payments also reduce retained earnings (C).

	Income Statement	損益計算書	After 15 活動15後	Act.16 活動16	After 16 活動16後
	Sales (Revenue)	売上高（営業収益）	227,638		227,638
−	Cost of Goods Sold	売上原価	125,750		125,750
=	Gross Margin	売上総利益	101,888	0	101,888
−	Selling, General & Administrative Expenses	販管費	55,250		55,250
=	Income from Operations	営業利益	46,638	0	46,638
+/−	Non-operating Profit/Expenses	営業外損益	−10,000		−10,000
−	Income Taxes	法人所得税等	10,991		10,991
=	Net Income	当期純利益	25,646	0	25,646

	Cash Flow Statement	キャッシュフロー計算書	After 15 活動15後	Act.16 活動16	After 16 活動16後
	Cash Receipts from Customers	売上収入	140,840		140,840
−	Cash Paid to Suppliers and Employees	経費の支払いによる支出	110,750		110,750
−	Income Taxes Paid	法人所得税等の支払い	0		0
=A	Cash Flows from Operating Activities	営業活動によるキャッシュフロー	30,090	0	30,090
−	Purchase of Property, Plant & Equipment	固定資産の取得	175,000		175,000
−	Purchase of Marketable Securities	金融資産の取得	0		0
=B	Cash Flows from Investing Activities	投資活動によるキャッシュフロー	−175,000	0	−175,000
	Increase in Debt	借入金・社債の増加	150,000		150,000
−	Interests Paid	利息支払い	10,000		10,000
−	Dividends Paid	配当支払い	0	[A] 10,000	10,000
+	Issuance of Common Stock	株式の発行	100,000		100,000
=C	Cash Flows from Financing Activities	財務活動によるキャッシュフロー	240,000	−10,000	230,000
A+B+C	Change in Cash	現金の増減額	95,090	−10,000	85,090

配当を支払う

利益が出ていますので,「昭和せんべい」の取締役会（実際にはあなた）は,
1株あたり 0.1 ドルの配当金を支払うことを決定し,株主（実際にはあなた）
に支払いました。「昭和せんべい」は 100,000 株を発行していますので,配当
金の総額は 10,000 ドルです。

● CFS で配当支払い 10,000 ドルを計上します（A）。

● BS の現金残高が減少します（B）。

● 配当支払いの分,利益剰余金が減少します（C）。

	Balance Sheet	貸借対照表	After 15 活動15後	Act.16 活動16	After 16 活動16後
	Cash	現金	95,090	−10,000	85,090
+	Marketable Securities	金融資産（有価証券）	0	B	0
+	Accounts Receivable	売上債権（売掛金）	78,798		78,798
+	Inventories	棚卸資産（在庫）	0		0
+	Prepaid Expenses	前払費用	0		0
+	Other Current Assets	その他流動資産	0		0
=	Current Assets	流動資産	173,888	−10,000	163,888
+	Property, Plant & Equipment	有形固定資産	166,750	0	166,750
+	Financial Investment	金融投資	0		0
+	Other Fixed Assets	その他固定資産	0		0
=	Total Assets	資産合計	340,638	−10,000	330,638
	Accounts Payable	仕入債務（買掛金）	40,000	0	40,000
+	Accrued Expenses	未払費用	14,000		14,000
+	Income Taxes Payable	未払法人所得税	10,991		10,991
+	Advanced Payment	前受金	0		0
+	Current Portion of Debt	短期社債・借入金	50,000		50,000
+	Other Current Liabilities	その他流動負債	0		0
=a	Current Liabilities	流動負債	114,991	0	114,991
	Long-term Debt	長期社債・借入金	100,000		100,000
+	Other Fixed Liabilities	その他固定負債	0		0
=b	Fixed Liabilities	固定負債	100,000	0	100,000
a+b=c	Total Liabilities	負債合計	214,991	0	214,991
	Capital Stock	資本金	100,000	0	100,000
+	Retained Earnings	利益剰余金	25,646	C −10,000	15,646
=d	Shareholders' Equity	株主資本合計	125,646	−10,000	115,646
c+d	Total Liabilities & Equity	負債及び資本合計	340,638	−10,000	330,638

One-point Lecture   Share Repurchase

Alternatively to dividends, a company can repurchase (buyback) its own shares as a measure to return cash to its shareholders.

Whereas dividends pay cash uniformly to all shareholders, share repurchases pay cash only to certain shareholders exchanging cash for shares.

For example, if a company repurchased 10,000 shares for $15 per share, $150,000 would be paid to shareholders, which reduces the number of shares by 10,000. The shares repurchased are recorded under shareholders' equity as a negative value, meaning we must decrease the value of shareholders' equity in the BS. The reacquired shares are then held by the company as treasury stock and can be sold again when the company requires funding in the future.

　企業が株主に資金を還元する方法としては，配当のほかに，株式を買い戻す「自社株買い」があります。

　配当が株主全員に均一的に現金を支払うのに対して，自社株買いでは，特定の株主のみに株式と引き換えに現金が支払われます。

　たとえば，会社が1株あたり15ドルで10,000株を買い戻すと，現金150,000ドルが株主に支払われ，流通する株式が10,000株減少することになります。買い戻された分の自社の株式は，株主資本にマイナスで計上され，株主資本の額は自社株買いを行った額の分だけ減少します。取得された株式は自己株式（金庫株とも呼ばれます）として企業によって保持され，企業が資金を必要とする場合は再度売り出されます。

Activity 15, 16: Application Exercise

A. Pay the $10,991 corporate income tax that was recorded in Activity 15.

B. Declare another dividend of $0.05 per share and pay these dividends to the company shareholders (the number of shares is 100,000).

How do the financial statements change in A and B, respectively?

Income Statement	損益計算書	14,15 Exercise A 14,15 応用問題 A	14,15 Exercise B 14,15 応用問題 B
Sales (Revenue)	売上高（営業収益）		
− Cost of Goods Sold	売上原価		
= Gross Margin	売上総利益	0	0
− Selling, General & Administrative Expenses	販管費		
= Income from Operations	営業利益	0	0
+/− Non-operating Profit/Expenses	営業外損益		
− Income Taxes	法人所得税等		
= Net Income	当期純利益	0	0

Cash Flow Statement	キャッシュフロー計算書	14,15 Exercise A 14,15 応用問題 A	14,15 Exercise B 14,15 応用問題 B
Cash Receipts from Customers	売上収入		
− Cash Paid to Suppliers and Employees	経費の支払いによる支出		
− Income Taxes Paid	法人所得税等の支払い	10,991	
=A Cash Flows from Operating Activities	営業活動によるキャッシュフロー	−10,991	0
− Purchase of Property, Plant & Equipment	固定資産の取得		
− Purchase of Marketable Securities	金融資産の取得		
=B Cash Flows from Investing Activities	投資活動によるキャッシュフロー	0	0
Increase in Debt	借入金・社債の増加	0	
− Interests Paid	利息支払い		
− Dividends Paid	配当支払い		5,000
+ Issuance of Common Stock	株式の発行		
=C Cash Flows from Financing Activities	財務活動によるキャッシュフロー	0	−5,000
A+B+C Change in Cash	現金の増減額	−10,991	−5,000

活動 15, 16：応用問題

A. 活動 15 で計上された 10,991 ドルの法人所得税を納めます。

B. 1 株あたり 0.05 ドルの配当を決定し，株主に支払います（株数は 100,000 株です）。

A，B それぞれで，財務三表はどのように変化しますか？

	Balance Sheet	貸借対照表	14,15 Exercise A 14,15 応用問題 A	14,15 Exercise B 14,15 応用問題 B
	Cash	現金	−10,991	−5,000
+	Marketable Securities	金融資産（有価証券）		
+	Accounts Receivable	売上債権（売掛金）		
+	Inventories	棚卸資産（在庫）		
+	Prepaid Expenses	前払費用		
+	Other Current Assets	その他流動資産		
=	Current Assets	流動資産	−10,991	−5,000
+	Property, Plant & Equipment	有形固定資産		0
+	Financial Investment	金融投資		
+	Other Fixed Assets	その他固定資産		
=	Total Assets	資産合計	−10,991	−5,000
	Accounts Payable	仕入債務（買掛金）	0	0
+	Accrued Expenses	未払費用		
+	Income Taxes Payable	未払法人所得税	−10,991	
+	Advanced Payment	前受金		
+	Current Portion of Debt	短期社債・借入金	0	
+	Other Current Liabilities	その他流動負債		
=a	Current Liabilities	流動負債	−10,991	0
	Long−term Debt	長期社債・借入金		
+	Other Fixed Liabilities	その他固定負債		
=b	Fixed Liabilities	固定負債	0	0
a+b=c	Total Liabilities	負債合計	−10,991	0
	Capital Stock	資本金	0	0
+	Retained Earnings	利益剰余金	0	−5,000
=d	Shareholders' Equity	株主資本合計	0	−5,000
c+d	Total Liabilities & Equity	負債及び資本合計	−10,991	−5,000

All the results of Showa Senbei's activities so far have been recorded in the BS, IS, and CFS as shown in the figures below.

However, how can we use these figures to evaluate a company's financial performance? What should we consider as potential risks in the future?

In order to examine them, many business professionals utilize effective techniques to conduct financial analysis. The next chapter will provide detail discussion on these financial analysis techniques.

Income Statement		損益計算書	After 16 活動16後
	Sales (Revenue)	売上高（営業収益）	227,638
−	Cost of Goods Sold	売上原価	125,750
=	Gross Margin	売上総利益	101,888
−	Selling, General & Administrative Expenses	販管費	55,250
=	Income from Operations	営業利益	46,638
+/−	Non-operating Profit/Expenses	営業外損益	−10,000
−	Income Taxes	法人所得税等	10,991
=	Net Income	当期純利益	25,646

Cash Flow Statement		キャッシュフロー計算書	After 16 活動16後
	Cash Receipts from Customers	売上収入	140,840
−	Cash Paid to Suppliers and Employees	経費の支払いによる支出	110,750
−	Income Taxes Paid	法人所得税等の支払い	0
=A	Cash Flows from Operating Activities	営業活動によるキャッシュフロー	30,090
−	Purchase of Property, Plant & Equipment	固定資産の取得	175,000
−	Purchase of Marketable Securities	金融資産の取得	0
=B	Cash Flows from Investing Activities	投資活動によるキャッシュフロー	−175,000
	Increase in Debt	借入金・社債の増加	150,000
−	Interests Paid	利息支払い	10,000
−	Dividends Paid	配当支払い	10,000
+	Issuance of Common Stock	株式の発行	100,000
=C	Cash Flows from Financing Activities	財務活動によるキャッシュフロー	230,000
A+B+C	Change in Cash	現金の増減額	85,090

「昭和せんべい」のこれまでの活動のすべての結果が以下の PL，BS，CFS のように記録されました。

それでは，これらの数値は財務業績として，どのように評価されるべきでしょうか。また将来的なリスクとして何を考えるべきでしょうか。

実務においては財務分析のためのいくつかの有効な手法が使われます。次の章ではこれらの手法について詳細に議論していきましょう。

	Balance Sheet	貸借対照表	After 16 活動16後
	Cash	現金	85,090
+	Marketable Securities	金融資産（有価証券）	0
+	Accounts Receivable	売上債権（売掛金）	78,798
+	Inventories	棚卸資産（在庫）	0
+	Prepaid Expenses	前払費用	0
+	Other Current Assets	その他流動資産	0
=	Current Assets	流動資産	163,888
+	Property, Plant & Equipment	有形固定資産	166,750
+	Financial Investment	金融投資	0
+	Other Fixed Assets	その他固定資産	0
=	Total Assets	資産合計	330,638
	Accounts Payable	仕入債務（買掛金）	40,000
+	Accrued Expenses	未払費用	14,000
+	Income Taxes Payable	未払法人所得税	10,991
+	Advanced Payment	前受金	0
+	Current Portion of Debt	短期社債・借入金	50,000
+	Other Current Liabilities	その他流動負債	0
=a	Current Liabilities	流動負債	114,991
	Long−term Debt	長期社債・借入金	100,000
+	Other Fixed Liabilities	その他固定負債	0
=b	Fixed Liabilities	固定負債	100,000
a+b=c	Total Liabilities	負債合計	214,991
	Capital Stock	資本金	100,000
+	Retained Earnings	利益剰余金	15,646
=d	Shareholders' Equity	株主資本合計	115,646
c+d	Total Liabilities & Equity	負債及び資本合計	330,638

Chapter 3

Constructing and Analyzing Financial Statements
What do the financial statements represent?

- This chapter introduces figures to evaluate the financial performance of a company in terms of profitability, efficiency, safety, and growth, by combining information from the different financial statements.

- It explores the actual calculation procedure for cash flow in practice known as the indirect method, and the actual bookkeeping procedure for accounting known as the double entry system.

- The latter part of this chapter shows how calculation results can vary depending on the country due to different accounting standards. Lastly, this chapter demonstrates the limitation of accounting by using examples from real companies.

第3章

財務諸表の構成と分析

財務三表は何を表わしているのか

★★★

● 本章では，財務諸表に記載されている情報を組みあわせて，利益率，効率性，安全性，成長率などの観点から企業の財務業績を評価するための数値を紹介します。

● 実際に実務において活用されている，間接法と呼ばれるキャッシュフローの計算方法や，複式簿記の仕訳といった会計処理の仕方についても理解していきます。

● 本章の後半では各国によって会計の基準が異なり，その結果計算数値が異なる可能性を理解し，最後に会計の限界についても，現実の企業の数値例を交えて紹介します。

Section

1 Financial Analysis

● Various Financial Measures

The numbers on a company's balance sheet, income statement, and cash flow statement can be combined and converted into valid measures that evaluate the state of a company's business.

There are many of these financial measures, including indicators that represent profit margins, asset efficiency, safety, growth, and so on, and these measures can be devised according to their purpose. The representative measures will be introduced in the following.

● Measure of Profitability

Profit margin is a measure of profitability indicating how much profit is generated out of sales.

ROA (Return on Assets) and **ROE (Return on Equity)** combines the IS and BS. ROA is calculated as profits divided by total assets, and ROE is calculated as profits divided by shareholders' equity.

Because ROA places total assets in the denominator, it shows how much return is generated from all of the assets a company uses, while ROE shows how much return is generated from shareholders' equity. These measures indicate how much capital (money) is utilized by the company, and how much profit is raised by them in percentages.

第1節 財務分析

● さまざまな財務評価指標

貸借対照表，損益計算書，およびキャッシュフロー計算書に記載される数値は，それらを組み合わせることにより企業の事業の状態を評価する有効な数値に変換できます。

財務指標と呼ばれるこれらの数値は数多く存在し，利益率，資産の効率性，安全性，成長率などを表わすさまざまな指標があります。さらにこれらの数値はその目的に応じていかようにも工夫が可能です。以下では代表的な指標を紹介していきます。

● 利益率を表わす指標

売上高利益率は売上高のうち利益がどれだけ生み出されているのかという収益性を示す指標です。

また，ROA（総資産利益率・総資本利益率）や，ROE（株主資本利益率）はPLとBSを統合した数値です。ROAは利益を総資産で割ることで求められ，ROEは利益を株主資本で割ることによって求められます。

ROAは分母に総資産をとるため，企業の使用しているすべての資産がどれだけのリターンを生み出しているのかを示し，一方でROEは，株主から調達した資本がどれだけのリターンを生み出しているのかを示します。これらの指標はどれだけの資本（お金）を使って，どれだけの利益を上げているのかをパーセント（％）で表わします。

Figure 3.1 Measure of Profitability

Measure	Formula	Meaning
Profit Margin	$\dfrac{\text{Profit}}{\text{Sales}}$	How much profit is earned out of sales?
ROA	$\dfrac{\text{Profit}}{\text{Total Assets}}$	How much profit is earned from all the assets used?
ROE	$\dfrac{\text{Profit}}{\text{Shareholders' Equity}}$	How much profit is earned from shareholders' equity?

The profit used in the profitability measures calculation often varies depending on the objective and is not uniform. Operating income, net income, or other types of profit can be used.

Net income, however, is most commonly used for ROE calculations. The total assets or shareholders' equity should be fundamentally based on a beginning balance, but the average of beginning and ending balance or simply ending balances are frequently used to calculate ROA and ROE in practice.

● Measure of Asset Efficiency

Asset turnover represents how efficiently a company's assets are used to generate its sales. It is calculated by dividing the sales by the total assets, indicating that the higher the value, the more efficiently the assets are used. Note that the asset turnover is usually around 1 (100%), and is normally not expressed in percentages.

Figure 3.2 Measure of Asset Efficiency

Measure	Formula	Meaning
Asset Turnover	$\dfrac{\text{Sales}}{\text{Total Assets}}$	How efficiently are a company's assets used to generate its sales?

図表 3.1 ▎ 利益率を表わす指標

指標	計算式	意味
売上高利益率	$\dfrac{利益}{売上高}$	売上に対してどれだけ利益を上げたか
ROA	$\dfrac{利益}{総資産}$	企業が使用するすべての資産に対してどれだけ利益を上げたか
ROE	$\dfrac{利益}{株主資本}$	株主から調達した資本に対してどれだけ利益を上げたか

　利益率指標の分子にどの利益を使用するのかは，その目的によって異なり，画一的ではありません。場合に応じて，営業利益，当期純利益，あるいはその他の指標が使われます。

　ROE の分子には当期純利益が使用されることがほとんどです。また，ROA の分母の総資産あるいは ROE の分母の株主資本は，本来的にはその期の初め（期首）の数値を使うべきですが，実務においては期首と期末の平均値（期中平均）や期末の値が使用されることも多くあります。

❷ 資産の効率性を表わす指標

　売上を生み出すために資産をどれだけ効率的に活用しているのかを示すのが総資産回転率です。総資産回転率は売上高を総資産で割って計算され，この値が高いほど効率性が高いことを示します。なおこの数値は通常 1 近辺（100%近辺）になることが多いので，%で表記することがあまりありません。

図表 3.2 ▎ 資産の効率性を表わす指標

指標	計算式	意味
総資産回転率	$\dfrac{売上高}{総資産}$	売上を生み出すために資産をどれだけ効率的に活用しているのか

⦿ Measure of Safety

Some measures indicates the safeness of a company. The **liability (to asset) ratio** represents how much liabilities a company utilizes out of the total assets. The opposite of the liability ratio is the **equity (to asset) ratio**, and the liability ratio plus the equity ratio is always equal to 1 by construction. A too high liability ratio derived from excessive debt, suggests a potential solvency risk. Conversely, a high equity ratio indicates a relatively low risk of bankruptcy.

On the other hand, a high liability ratio also means that shareholders who are owners of the company are relying heavily on other people's funds, so they do not have to provide as much of their own money. It is said that running a business with a less capital is efficient, which is called the leverage effect or the financial leverage.

Furthermore, the **current ratio** indicates the safeness of a company in the near future, which is calculated as the current assets divided by the current liabilities. To be classified as current assets they have to turn into cash within 1 year, whereas current liabilities are classified as liabilities that must be repaid within a year. Therefore, a current ratio exceeding 1 demonstrates that the liabilities to be repaid within 1 year can be covered by the assets that turn into cash within the same year.

The **quick ratio** is a more stringent version of the current ratio. Current assets consist of cash, marketable securities, accounts receivables, inventories and so on. Among them, particularly more cashable assets such as cash, marketable securities, and accounts receivables are called quick assets. The quick ratio is calculated as the quick asset by the current liabilities, which represents whether a highly cashable asset can cover the liabilities to be repaid within one year.

Basically, the higher the current ratio and the quick ratio, the safer the company is regarded.

● 安全性を表わす指標

　次に，企業の安全性を表わす指標をいくつか紹介します。**負債総資産比率**は企業が総資産のうちどれだけ負債を活用しているのかを表わします。そしてこの反対が**株主資本総資産比率**であり，構造上，負債総資産比率＋株主資本総資産比率＝１となります。負債総資産比率が高すぎるということは，負債が多いということですから，潜在的な支払い能力に関する危険性が示唆されることになります。反対に，株主資本総資産比率が高ければ，企業の倒産に対する危険度は比較的低いといえます。

　一方で，負債総資産比率が高いということは，会社の所有者である株主からしてみれば，他人の資金を活用している度合いが高いということであり，自分の拠出する資金が少なくて済むことを意味します。小さい資金で事業ができるのであれば効率は高く，この効果のことをレバレッジ（てこ）効果（財務レバレッジ）と呼びます。

　また，より短期的な企業の安全性を示す数値に**流動比率**があります。流動比率は流動資産を流動負債の額で割った数値です。流動資産は１年以内に現金に変わる資産であり，流動負債は１年以内に返済すべき負債です。そのため，流動資産が流動負債を上回る，つまり流動比率が１以上であるということは，１年以内に返済すべき負債を１年以内に現金に変わる資産でまかなえることを表わします。

　当座比率は流動比率の考え方をさらに厳格にした数値です。流動資産は現金，有価証券，売上債権，在庫などを含みますが，この中でも特に換金性の高い，現金，有価証券，売上債権，は当座資産と呼ばれます。この当座資産を流動負債で割った数値が当座比率です。１年以内に返済すべき負債をより換金性の高い資産のみでまかなえるのかどうかを表わしています。

　基本的には流動比率・当座比率は高いほど，その会社は安全だと判断されます。

Figure 3.3 | Measure of Safety

Measure	Formula	Meaning
Liability Ratio	$\dfrac{\text{Total Liabilities}}{\text{Total Assets}}$	How much of the assets are covered by liabilities?
Equity Ratio	$\dfrac{\text{Shareholders' Equity}}{\text{Total Assets}}$	How much of the assets are covered by shareholders' equity?
Current Ratio	$\dfrac{\text{Current Assets}}{\text{Current Liabilities}}$	Can short-term financial demand be covered with short-term assets?
Quick Ratio	$\dfrac{\text{Quick Assets}}{\text{Current Liabilities}}$	Can short-term financial demand be covered with highly cashable assets?

○ Measure of Growth

Financial measures representing growth are expressed by calculating changes over time. **Sales growth** represents how much the business expands over a period of time.

Profit growth is calculated similarly. As with profitability measures, a profit focused on growth depends on your purpose.

Figure 3.4 | Measure of Growth

Measure	Formula	Meaning
Sales Growth	$\dfrac{\text{Sales in Current Period} - \text{Sales in Previous Period}}{\text{Sales in Previous Period}}$ $= \dfrac{\text{Sales in Current Period}}{\text{Sales in Previous Period}} - 1$	How much a business expands over the period?
Profit Growth	$\dfrac{\text{Profit in Current Period} - \text{Profit in Previous Period}}{\text{Profit in Previous Period}}$ $= \dfrac{\text{Profit in Current Period}}{\text{Profit in Previous Period}} - 1$	How much profit increases over the period?

図表 3.3 ┃ 安全性を表わす指標

指標	計算式	意味
負債総資産比率	$\dfrac{負債}{総資産}$	資産のうちどれだけを負債でまかなっているか
株主資本総資産比率	$\dfrac{株主資本}{総資産}$	資産のうちどれだけを株主資本でまかなっているか
流動比率	$\dfrac{流動資産}{流動負債}$	短期的な資金需要に短期的な資産で対応できるか
当座比率	$\dfrac{当座資産}{流動負債}$	短期的な資金需要に換金性の高い資産で対応できるか

❍ 成長を表わす指標

　成長を表わす財務数値は，時系列的な変化を計算することで表わされます。売上成長率は事業が一定期間においてどれだけ拡大・伸張したのかを示すものです。

　利益成長率も同様の方法で計算されます。利益率の計算と同じように，どの利益を使用するのかは目的によって変わってきます。

図表 3.4 ┃ 成長率を表わす指標

指標	計算式	意味
売上成長率	$\dfrac{当期売上高-前期売上高}{前期売上高}$ $=\dfrac{当期売上高}{前期売上高}-1$	企業・事業がどれだけ拡大・伸張したのか
利益成長率	$\dfrac{当期の利益-前期の利益}{前期の利益}$ $=\dfrac{当期の利益}{前期の利益}-1$	利益がどれだけ拡大・伸張したのか

● DuPont Formula

DuPont, a chemical company, has integrated these metrics into its management control system. The system and technique are well known as the DuPont formula.

The DuPont formula divides ROE into three parts, profit margin, asset turnover, and equity ratio.

$$ROE = Profit\ Margin \times Asset\ Turnover / Equity\ Ratio$$

$$\frac{Profit}{Shareholders'\ Equity} = \frac{Profit}{Sales} \times \frac{Sales}{Total\ Assets} / \frac{Shareholders'\ Equity}{Total\ Asstes}$$

The equation indicates that for a company to achieve a higher ROE they should increase profits from sales, improve asset efficiency, and rely more on liabilities (relatively reducing shareholders' equity and increasing the financial leverage).

The following part of the equation,

$$\frac{Profit}{Sales} \times \frac{Sales}{Total\ Assets}$$

corresponds to ROA, so with the identical ROA, a company utilizing more debt and fewer shareholders' equity can enjoy a higher ROE (strictly speaking, interest expenses on debt slightly reduces the profit of the company). The reliance on debt deteriorates a company's financial safety, but the leverage effect improves its profitablity.

● デュポン公式

化学会社のデュポンは以上のような指標を統合した分析手法を経営管理に取り入れました。その手法はデュポン公式として普及しています。

デュポン公式は，ROE を売上高利益率，総資産回転率，株主資本総資産比率の3つに分解する式です。すなわち，ROE は以下のように分解されます。

$$ROE = 売上高利益率 × 総資産回転率 ÷ 株主資本総資産比率$$

$$\frac{利益}{株主資本} = \frac{利益}{売上高} × \frac{売上高}{総資産} ÷ \frac{株主資本}{総資産}$$

この式は，企業が高い ROE を達成するためには，売上高から上がる利益を増やし，資産の効率性を高め，かつ負債への依存を増やす（相対的に株主資本を減らして財務レバレッジを高める）ことが有効であることを示しています。

なお，この式のうち，

$$\frac{利益}{売上高} × \frac{売上高}{総資産}$$

の部分は ROA にあたりますから，同じ ROA であれば，なるべく少ない株主資本でより多くの負債を活用する企業ほど ROE は高まることになります（厳密にいえば，負債の利息費用により企業の利益は若干減少します）。負債の活用によって企業の財務安全性は低くなりますが，一方でレバレッジ効果により企業の利益率が高まるのです。

● Financial Results of Showa Senbei

Figure 3.5 calculates the financial measures of Showa Senbei based on its financial performance discussed in the previous chapter. All profitability measures use net income for the calculation in the figure.

As a side note, the growth rate of Showa Senbei is not shown because it has only been performing for one year.

Additionally, since the current assets at the end of the fiscal year included only cash and accounts receivables, the current ratio and the quick ratio of Showa Senbei generate the same value. A company usually holds other current assets such as inventories at the end of the fiscal year, therefore, the current ratio is likely smaller than the quick ratio.

Figure 3.5 ▌ Financial Results of Showa Senbei

Measure	Formula	
Profit Margin	Net Income/Sales	11.3%
ROA (Return on Assets)	Net Income/Total Assets	7.8%
ROE (Return on Equity)	Net Income/Shareholers' Equity	22.2%
Asset Turnover	Sales/Total Assets	0.7
Liability Ratio	Total Liabilities/Total Assets	65.0%
Equity Ratio	Shareholers' Equity/Total Assets	35.0%
Current Ratio	Current Assets/Current Liabilities	1.43
Quick Ratio	(Cash+Securities+Receivables)/Current Liabilities	1.43

● 「昭和せんべい」の財務数値

　図表 3.5 は前章で紹介した「昭和せんべい」の業績に基づいて，これまで紹介した指標を計算したものです。なお，ここでは利益率の計算はすべて当期純利益を使用しています。

　なお，「昭和せんべい」の業績は 1 年間しかありませんので，成長率は計算できません。

　また，「昭和せんべい」の期末の流動資産は現金と売上債権だけですので，流動比率と当座比率は同じ値となっています。通常の企業は期末に棚卸資産など他の流動資産を保有していますので，流動比率と当座比率は異なり，当座比率のほうが小さい値となるはずです。

図表 3.5 ┃ 「昭和せんべい」の財務数値

指標	計算方法	
売上高利益率	当期純利益／売上高	11.3%
ROA（総資産利益率）	当期純利益／資産合計	7.8%
ROE（株主資本利益率）	当期純利益／株主資本	22.2%
総資産回転率	売上高／資産合計	0.7
負債総資産比率	負債合計／資産合計	65.0%
株主資本総資産比率	株主資本／資産合計	35.0%
流動比率	流動資産／流動負債	1.43
当座比率	(現金＋金融資産＋売上債権)／流動負債	1.43

Common Size Financial Statements

Common size financial statements represent each accounting item as a ratio. They show how a company incurs costs, makes profit, takes advantage of capital to make the profit, and what type of assets it owns in percentages.

The common size income statement represents all items on the IS as a ratio to sales, and the common size balance sheet represents all items on the BS as a ratio to total assets (total liabilities plus equity). All numbers that are converted to percentages and standardized eliminates the impact of size. This creates more useful data for comparing cost structures, and assets and capital structures between companies of different sizes and helps analyze the historical trend of the structures over time.

Figure 3.6 shows the common size financial statements for Showa Senbei.

Figure 3.6 | Common Size Financial Statements for Showa Senbei

Common Size Income Statement

Sales Revenue	100.0%
Cost of Goods Sold	55.2%
Gross Margin	44.8%
Selling, General & Administrative Expenses	24.3%
Income from Operations	20.5%
Non-operating Profit/Expenses	−4.4%
Income Taxes	4.8%
Net Income	11.3%

Common Size Balance Sheet

Cash	25.7%
Marketable Securities	0.0%
Accounts Receivable	23.8%
Inventories	0.0%
Prepaid Expenses	0.0%
Other Current Assets	0.0%
Current Assets	49.6%
Property, Plant & Equipment	50.4%
Financial Investment	0.0%
Other Fixed Assets	0.0%
Total Assets	100.0%
Accounts Payable	12.1%
Accrued Expenses	4.2%
Income Taxes Payable	3.3%
Advanced Payment	0.0%
Current Portion of Debt	15.1%
Other Current Liabilities	0.0%
Current Liabilities	34.8%
Long-term Debt	30.2%
Other Fixed Liabilities	0.0%
Fixed Liabilities	30.2%
Total Liabilities	65.0%
Capital Stock	30.2%
Retained Earnings	4.7%
Shareholders' Equity	35.0%
Total Liabilities & Equity	100.0%

標準化財務諸表とは各会計項目を比率で表わすものです。企業がどのように
コストをかけて利益を上げているのか，またその利益を上げるためにどのよう
に資本を活用しているのか，どのような資産を有しているのかを％で示します。

標準化損益計算書は損益計算書上のすべての項目を売上高に対する比率とし
て表わし，標準化貸借対照表は貸借対照表上のすべての項目を総資産（負債・
株主資本合計）に対する比率で表わします。数値を％に変換することにより，
金額規模の影響が排除され，規模の異なる企業間のコスト構造や資産・資本構
造を比較したり，時系列的な構造の変化を分析することができるようになりま
す。

図表 3.6 は「昭和せんべい」の標準化財務諸表を示しています。

図表 3.6 ┃ 「昭和せんべい」の標準化財務諸表

標準化損益計算書

売上高（営業収益）	100.0%
売上原価	55.2%
売上総利益	44.8%
販管費	24.3%
営業利益	20.5%
営業外損益	−4.4%
法人所得税等	4.8%
当期純利益	11.3%

標準化貸借対照表

現金	25.7%
金融資産（有価証券）	0.0%
売上債権（売掛金）	23.8%
棚卸資産（在庫）	0.0%
前払費用	0.0%
その他流動資産	0.0%
流動資産	49.6%
有形固定資産	50.4%
金融投資	0.0%
その他固定資産	0.0%
資産合計	100.0%
仕入債務（買掛金）	12.1%
未払費用	4.2%
未払法人所得税	3.3%
前受金	0.0%
短期社債・借入金	15.1%
その他流動負債	0.0%
流動負債	34.8%
長期社債・借入金	30.2%
その他固定負債	0.0%
固定負債	30.2%
負債合計	65.0%
資本金	30.2%
利益剰余金	4.7%
株主資本合計	35.0%
負債及び資本合計	100.0%

2 How Cash Flow is Calculated

● Actual Cash Flow Statement

As discussed in the first chapter, a cash flow statement shows cash movements over a period divided into three categories: operating, investing, and financing activities. In fact, there are two approaches to display cash flow from operating activities, and most companies use a different format than Showa Senbei's CFS described in Chapter 2.

The displayed format introduced until now is called the **direct method**. This method records every time cash is received and paid resembling a retail store's cash register. The alternative method is known as the **indirect method**.

The name of the indirect method stems from its recording process. The indirect method does not record the movement of cash "directly" as the direct method does, but "indirectly" captures the movement of cash through the IS and BS.

The indirect method starts its calculation for operating cash flow with the accounting profit or IS and then deals with various items changing on the BS and depreciation. Investing cash flow and financing cash flow are derived from the information on the BS. Of course, either method calculates identical figures because they have no effect on the cash on hand. Therefore, the final calculation results are unchanged, but the calculation process is different.

● Cash Flow Calculation with Indirect Method

Let's take a closer look at the calculation process using the indirect method for operating cash flow. Operating cash flow is calculated by adding back depreciation to the profit and then deducting the increase in **working capital**.

Operating Cash Flow = Profit + Depreciation − Increase in Working Capital

Why is the cash movement happening through the operating activities gauged by

第2節 キャッシュフローの計算方法

◉ 実際のキャッシュフロー計算書

　第1章で学んだように，キャッシュフロー計算書は，一定期間における現金の動きを，営業活動，投資活動，財務活動の3つのカテゴリーに分けて示したものでした。実はこのうち営業活動によるキャッシュフローには2通りの表示の仕方があり，ほとんどの企業は，第2章で示した「昭和せんべい」のキャッシュフロー計算書とは異なる形式を使用しています。

　これまで紹介してきたキャッシュフロー計算書の表示形式は**直接法**と呼ばれます。これは，商店のレジのように，入金と出金のたびに1つひとつ記録していく方式です。もう1つの方法は，**間接法**と呼ばれるものです。

　なぜ間接法というのかというと，間接法は，直接法のように現金の動きを「直接的に」記録するのではなく，損益計算書と貸借対照表の記録を介して「間接的に」現金の動きをとらえるからです。

　間接法では，営業キャッシュフローは，会計上の利益・PL からスタートし，そこに BS 項目の増減額や減価償却費を調整して計算されます。また，投資キャッシュフローと財務キャッシュフローは BS の情報から作成します。当然ですが，どちらの方法をとっても手元の現金が変わるわけではないので，最終的な計算結果は同じになります。結果は同じなのですが計算プロセスが異なるのです。

◉ 間接法によるキャッシュフローの計算

　間接法の営業キャッシュフローの計算をもう少し具体的に見ていきましょう。営業キャッシュフローは以下のように，利益に減価償却費を足し戻し，その後**運転資本**の増額を差し引いて計算します。

営業キャッシュフロー＝利益＋減価償却費－運転資本増額

　ではなぜこの式で営業活動において生じる現金の動きがとらえられるので

the equation?

● Add Back Depreciation

Depreciation is the distribution of expenses that relates the fixed assets to each period they are available. Depreciation is an accounting expense, but it is not associated with the cash expenditure during the period because cash payments have already occurred at the time the asset was purchased. However, when calculating cash flow, it is necessary to add depreciation back to the profit because depreciation is deducted as a part of the costs or expenses during profit calculation.

● Deduct an Increase in Working Capital

The impact of increasing or decreasing working capital on cash may be a little confusing. Working capital, unlike fixed assets such as equipment, are always replaced or working. They occur along with operating activities and are necessary for the operation.

Working capital is expressed as the difference between the sum of current assets from operating activities (such as accounts receivables and inventories), and the sum of current liabilities incurred from operating activities (such as accounts payables). This is also known as **net working capital**.

Working capital = Accounts Receivables, Inventories, Prepaid Expenses, etc.
— Accounts Payables, Accrued Expenses, Income Tax Payables, Advance Payment, etc.

Liabilities from financial institutions such as borrowings and corporate bonds (or debt) are related to financial activities (instead of being related to operating activities), therefore it is not incorporated in the working capital calculation.

Since working capital is required for operating activities, an increase in working capital means the investment of additional funds. This increase negatively impacts cash flow, while a decrease in working capital has a positive impact on cash flow.

しょうか。

● 減価償却費を足し戻す

　減価償却費は，固定資産に関する費用を，それが使用できる各期間に配分するものです。減価償却費は会計上の費用ですが，その期において現金の支出があるわけではありません。現金支出はすでに資産の購入時点で発生しているからです。しかし，利益算出の際には，減価償却費は費用の一部として差し引かれているため，キャッシュフローを計算する際には，利益に減価償却費を足し戻す必要があります。

● 運転資本増額を差し引く

　運転資本の増減が現金に与える影響については，少しわかりにくいかもしれません。運転資本は，設備などの固定資産と異なり，常に中身が入れ替わっている資本です。営業活動に伴って発生し，営業活動を行う上で必要な資本といえます。

　運転資本は売掛金などの売上債権と棚卸資産（在庫）といった，現金以外の流動資産の合計と，仕入債務などの営業活動に伴って発生する流動負債の合計の差として表わされます。**正味運転資本**とも呼ばれます。

運転資本＝売上債権，棚卸資産，前払費用など
　　　　－仕入債務，未払費用，未払法人所得税，前受金など

　借入金や社債などの金融機関から資金調達に伴う負債は営業活動ではなく財務活動に伴う負債ですので，運転資本の計算には含みません。

　運転資本は営業活動に必要な資金ですので，運転資本の増加は追加的な資金の投入を意味します。運転資本の増加はキャッシュフローにマイナスの影響を，運転資本の減少はキャッシュフローにプラスの影響を与えます。そのため，

Therefore, the increase in working capital must be deducted to calculate cash flow.

For example, suppose you earn $100 in sales, which increases the profit by $100. If you receive the payment at that time, the cash flow is also positive $100, and the profit and cash flow are equivalent.

However, if it is a sale on credit and you have to wait for cash collection until a later date, the profit becomes positive $100, while cash flow remains 0 because you do not receive cash. This difference is accounted for under accounts receivable in the BS, and since accounts receivable constitutes working capital, the working capital increases by $100. This results in a cash flow of $0, which can be calculated by deducting the increase in working capital from the profit in the following equation.

$$\text{Cashflow } 0 = \text{Profit } 100 - \text{Increase in Working Capital } 100$$

An increase in current assets, such as accounts receivable, negatively affects cash flow because it signifies cash retention. On the other hand, a decrease in current assets means cash collection, which has a positive impact on cash flow.

Conversely, an increase in current liabilities, such as accounts payable, means raising cash, which positively impacts cash flow. Contrarily, a decrease in current liabilities means the cash has been repaid, which negatively impacts the company's cash flow.

These relationships are summarized in Figure 3.7.

Figure 3.7 | Effects of Working Capital on Cash Flow

Item	Change	Nature	Impact on CF
Accounts Receivable, Inventories, Prepaid Expenses, etc.	Increase	Cash Retention	Negative
	Decrease	Cash Collection	Positive
Accounts Payable, Accrued Expenses, Income Tax Payable, Advanced Payments, etc.	Increase	Raising Cash	Positive
	Decrease	Repayment of Cash	Negative

キャッシュフローを計算するためには，運転資本の増加額も差し引く必要があるのです。

たとえば，100 ドルの売上があったとしましょう。利益への影響はプラス100 ドルです。もし，その時点で代金を受け取ったのであれば，キャッシュフローもプラス 100 ドルということで利益とキャッシュフローは一致します。

しかし，この取引が掛け売りによって行われ，代金回収は後日だとしましょう。利益は 100 ドルですが現金は受け取っていませんのでキャッシュフローは0 ドルです。この差額分は BS の売上債権として計上されます。そして売上債権は運転資本ですので運転資本が 100 ドル増加しています。ここで，キャッシュフローは 0 でしたが，これは以下のように利益から運転資本の増額を差し引くことによって計算できるのです。

$$キャッシュフロー0 ＝利益100 －運転資本増100$$

売上債権のような流動資産の増加は資金の滞留を意味するので，キャッシュフローにマイナスの影響があります。一方で，これらの減少は資金の回収を意味し，キャッシュフローにプラスの影響があるのです。

逆に，仕入債務のような流動負債の増加は資金の調達を意味するので，キャッシュフローにプラスの影響があります。一方で，これらの減少は資金の返済を意味し，キャッシュフローにマイナスの影響があるのです。

この関係を図表 3.7 にまとめています。

図表 3.7 ▎運転資本のキャッシュフローへの影響

項目	変化	性質	CF への影響
売上債権，棚卸資産，前払費用など	増加	資金の滞留	マイナス
	減少	資金の回収	プラス
仕入債務，未払費用，未払法人所得税，前受金など	増加	資金の調達	プラス
	減少	資金の返済	マイナス

Figure 3.8 shows the cash flow statement of Showa Senbei with the indirect method. Please confirm that the change in cash is the same on the the CFS as it is with the direct method shown in Chapter 2 (inserted again as Figure 3.9), notwithstanding the calculation process of operating cash flow is different.

Figure 3.8 | Cash Flow Statement with Indirect Method

	Net Income	25,646
+	Depreciation	8,250
	Increase in Accounts Receivable	78,798
+	Increase in Inventories	0
+	Increase in Prepaid Expenses	0
−	Increase in Accounts Payable	40,000
−	Increase in Accrued Expenses	14,000
−	Increase in Income Taxes Payable	10,991
− =	Increase in Working Capital	13,806
=	(1) Cash Flows from Operating Activities	20,090
−	Purchase of Property, Plant & Equipment	175,000
−	Purchase of Marketable Securities	0
=	(2) Cash Flows from Investing Activities	−175,000
	Increase in Debt	150,000
−	Dividends Paid	10,000
+	Issuance of Common Stock	100,000
=	(3) Cash Flows from Financing Activities	240,000
(1) + (2) + (3)	Change in Cash	85,090
	Beginning Cash	0
	Ending Cash	85,090

◉ 「昭和せんべい」のキャッシュフロー計算書

　図表3.8は「昭和せんべい」のキャッシュフロー計算書を間接法で示したものです。第2章で示した直接法での計算（図表3.9として再掲）とは営業キャッシュフローの計算過程は異なっていても，現金の増減額は同じであることを確認してください。

図表 3.8 ┃ 間接法によるキャッシュフロー計算書

		当期純利益		25,646
+		減価償却費		8,250
		売上債権（売掛金）	の増加	78,798
+		棚卸資産（在庫）	の増加	0
+		前払費用	の増加	0
−		仕入債務（買掛金）	の増加	40,000
−		未払費用	の増加	14,000
−		未払法人所得税	の増加	10,991
−	=	運転資本の増加		13,806
=	(1)	営業活動によるキャッシュフロー		20,090
	−	固定資産の取得		175,000
	−	金融資産の取得		0
	=	(2) 投資活動によるキャッシュフロー		−175,000
		借入金・社債の増加		150,000
	−	配当支払い		10,000
	+	株式の発行		100,000
	=	(3) 財務活動によるキャッシュフロー		240,000
(1) + (2) + (3)		現金増減額		85,090
		期首現金残高		0
		期末現金残高		85,090

Figure 3.9 | Cash Flow Statement with Direct Method

	Cash Receipts from Customers	140,840
—	Cash Paid to Suppliers and Employees	110,750
—	Income Taxes Paid	0
= A	Cash Flows from Operating Activities	30,090
—	Purchase of Property, Plant & Equipment	175,000
—	Purchase of Marketable Securities	0
= B	Cash Flows from Investing Activities	−175,000
	Increase in Debt	150,000
—	Interests Paid	10,000
—	Dividends Paid	10,000
+	Issuance of Common Stock	100,000
= C	Cash Flows from Financing Activities	230,000
A + B + C	Change in Cash	85,090

Please note that cash flow from operating activities and cash flow from financing activities differ by $10,000. This is because interest payments are included when calculating net income (so they are not included in the cash flow from financing activities). Given its nature, interest paid should be considered as a part of cash flow from financing activities, but many accounting standards allow it to be included in cash flow from operating activities as an exception. The indirect methods that start calculations from profit frequently incorporate interest paid in cash flow from operating activities.

図表 3.9 ┃ 直接法によるキャッシュフロー計算書

	売上収入	140,840
―	経費の支払いによる支出	110,750
―	法人所得税等の支払い	0
＝ A	営業活動によるキャッシュフロー	30,090
―	固定資産の取得	175,000
―	金融資産の取得	0
＝ B	投資活動によるキャッシュフロー	−175,000
	借入金・社債の増加	150,000
―	利息支払い	10,000
―	配当支払い	10,000
＋	株式の発行	100,000
＝ C	財務活動によるキャッシュフロー	230,000
A＋B＋C	現金の増減額	85,090

　なお，営業活動によるキャッシュフローと財務活動によるキャッシュフローが 10,000 ドルずつ異なっています。この理由は利息の支払い額が利益の計算に含まれているからです（そのため財務活動によるキャッシュフローには含めていません）。その性質を考えると，本来，利息支払いは財務活動によるキャッシュフローの一部と考えるべきですが，多くの会計基準では例外的に営業活動によるキャッシュフローに含めてもいいことになっています。特に利益から計算をスタートする間接法においては，利息支払い額は営業活動によるキャッシュフローに含めて計算されることが多いのです。

○ Cash Flow Analysis

Operating CF, investing CF, and financing CF suggest the stage where a business is currently operating in.

Operating CF is negative during a start-up period just after the business is founded, but it is expected to turn positive during the growth and mature periods, then turn negative in a decline period.

Investing CF will be hugely negative during a growth period when the speed of business expansion is significant, and it will turn positive as funds are withdrawn from the business during a state of decline.

Financing CF is positive during the start-up and growth periods because businesses require money for growth, but will be negative during the mature period when operating CF is stably generated and expenditure for growth is limited. This is because a business starts to return cash to capital providers during this stage of maturity. Furthermore, financing CF will be more negative than investing CF in the later stages of maturity (refer to Figure 3.10).

It is often difficult to judge the stage of a business because of temporary increases in expenditures or non-recurring events, but it is possible to outline the status of businesses based on the sign of the three cash flow categories alone.

Figure 3.10 | Relationship between Business Stage and Cash Flow

Stage	Start-up	Growth	Mature	Decline
Operating CF	Negative	Positive	Positive	Negative
Investing CF	Negative	(Significantly) Negative	Negative	From negative to positive
Financing CF	Positive	Positive	Negative, more negative than investing CF in a later period	Negative

● キャッシュフロー分析

　営業キャッシュフロー，投資キャッシュフロー，財務キャッシュフローの値
は，その事業がどのようなステージにいるのかを示唆してくれます。

　営業キャッシュフローは，事業の初期段階の創業期にはマイナスですが，成
長期にプラスに転じ，成熟期を経て，衰退期にはマイナスになると考えられま
す。

　投資キャッシュフローは事業の拡大スピードが大きい成長期に多額のマイナ
スとなり，衰退期は事業からの資金を回収するのでプラスに転じるでしょう。

　財務キャッシュフローは資金が必要な創業期・成長期はプラスですが，成熟
期に入って安定的に営業キャッシュフローが稼ぎ出せ，また成長への投資がそ
れほど必要にならなくなるとマイナスになると考えられます。資金提供者への
資金還元が進むからです。特に成熟期の後期には財務キャッシュフローは投資
キャッシュフローを上回るマイナス額になるでしょう（図表3.10）。

　もちろん一時的な支出や，非経常的なイベントがキャッシュフローに影響を
与えることもあるので一概に事業ステージを判断することは難しい場合も多い
です。しかし，3つのキャッシュフロー分類の符号からだけでも，事業の状況
を概観することは可能なのです。

図表 3.10 ┃ 事業ステージとキャッシュフローの関係

ステージ	創業期	成長期	成熟期	衰退期
営業 キャッシュフロー	マイナス	プラス	プラス	マイナス
投資 キャッシュフロー	マイナス	大きな マイナス	マイナス	マイナスか らプラスへ
財務 キャッシュフロー	プラス	プラス	マイナス，やが て投資CFを上回 るマイナス	マイナス

③ Double Entry System

● Recording without Mistakes

Chapter 2 confirmed how Showa Senbei's business activities are recorded in the three financial statements. Financial accounting mandates how each activity affects each financial statement, and record it in the appropriate item with an accurate amount. However, there is a chance of unintentional input errors or missing entries.

Therefore, a company is required to use a systemic method to reduce potential errors called the **double entry (bookkeeping) system** to prepare financial statements.

● What is the Double Entry System?

In the double entry system, every activity generates more than one entry, which contains a component of **"debit"** on the left and a component of **"credit"** on the right. The debit and credit for each transaction are always equivalent, therefore the total of debit and credit are also equivalent. Because of this, they are used to prepare accurate and proper financial statements. Moreover, since everything in the double entry system is consistent, it can prevent accounting fraud.

In financial accounting, any activity can result in changes in assets, liabilities, shareholders' equity, sales (revenue), and expenses.

Of these, assets, liabilities, and shareholders' equity are components of the BS, with assets located on the left or debit side of the BS, and liabilities and shareholders' equity on the right or credit side of the BS. Therefore, increasing assets is recorded as debit, decreasing assets is recorded as credit, increasing liabilities and shareholders' equity is recorded as a credit, and decreasing liabilities and shareholders' equity is recorded as debit.

Sales (revenue) and expenses are components of the IS, and are tied with shareholders' equity. It creates a relationship where an increase in sales increases

第3節 複式簿記

● 間違いのない記録方法

　第2章では，「昭和せんべい」の事業活動が財務三表にどのように記録されるのかを確認しました。財務会計においては，それぞれの活動が財務諸表1つひとつにどのような影響があるのかを確認し，適切な場所に適切な額を記録する必要があります。しかし，うっかり間違いをしてしまったり，記入漏れが生じたりする可能性もあるでしょう。

　そのため，企業が財務諸表を作成する際には，**複式簿記**というシステマチックで間違いの起こりにくい方法を使用することが義務付けられています。

● 複式簿記とは

　複式簿記は，すべての活動を左側「**借方（かりかた）**」と右側「**貸方（かしかた）**」という複数で記録します。複式簿記のルール上，各取引の借方は貸方と常に一致し，最終的に借方と貸方の合計額は常に一致するので，正確で間違いのない財務諸表の作成が可能になります。また，複式簿記では必ずすべてつじつまが合わなければならないので，会計不正を防ぐ効果も期待できるのです。

　財務会計においては，いかなる活動も資産，負債，株主資本（純資産），売上（収益），費用のいずれかの変化をもたらします。

　このうち，資産，負債，株主資本はBSの要素であり，資産はBSの左側つまり借方，負債と株主資本はBSの右側つまり貸方に位置しています。それにあわせて，複式簿記では資産の増加は借方，資産の減少は貸方に記録し，負債と株主資本の増加は貸方，負債と株主資本の減少は借方に記録します。

　また，売上（収益），費用はPLの要素ですが，売上（収益）の増加は株主資本を増加させ，費用の増加は株主資本を減少させます。そのため，売上（収

shareholders' equity, and an increase in expenses decreases shareholders' equity. Therefore, an increase in sales is recorded as a credit, and a decrease in sales is recorded as a debit. Conversely, an increase in expenses is recorded as a debit, and a decrease in expenses is recorded as a credit.

Figure 3.11 summarizes the rule of double entry.

Figure 3.11 | Rule of Double Entry

Debit	Credit
Increase in Assets	Decrease in Assets
Decrease in Liabilities	Increase in Liabilities
Decrease in Shareholders' Equity	Increase in Shareholders' Equity
Incurring Expenses	Generating Sales (Revenue)

Classifying the contents of an accounting transaction into debit and credit categories and recording them is known as a journal entry or **journalizing**. All accounting transaction activities are debited and credited in the double entry system.

● Example of Double Entry

Let's review some activities of Showa Senbei and record them in the double entry system.

Double Entry **Activity 0: Found Showa Senbei Corporation**

In Activity 0, you invested $100,000 in cash on hand to establish Showa Senbei. Showa Senbei increased its capital stock in shareholders' equity, and cash in assets. Therefore, debit and credit are entered as follows:

Debit	Credit
Cash 100,000	Capital Stock 100,000

益）の増加は貸方に，売上（収益）の減少は借方に記録します。逆に費用の増加は借方に，費用の減少は貸方に記録します。

図表 3.11 はこのような複式簿記の記録方法をまとめています。

図表 3.11 ┃ 複式簿記での記録方法

借　方	貸　方
資産の増加	資産の減少
負債の減少	負債の増加
株主資本の減少	株主資本の増加
費用の発生	売上（収益）の発生

会計取引の内容を「借方」と「貸方」の左右に分類して，記録することを「仕訳」といいます。複式簿記では，すべての活動を借方，貸方に記録していきます。

● 複式簿記の例

「昭和せんべい」の活動のいくつかを複式簿記で記録して確認しましょう。

複式簿記 活動 0：「昭和せんべい」設立

活動 0 では「昭和せんべい」の設立にあたり，あなたは手持ちの現金100,000 ドルを出資しました。「昭和せんべい」は株主資本の資本金を増やし，現金という資産を増やしました。そのため複式簿記では，以下のように仕訳されます。

借　方	貸　方
現　金　　100,000	資本金　　100,000

Double Entry Activity 6: Book Depreciation and Manufacturing Overheads

Activity 6 recorded a depreciation of $6,250 and light and heat expenses of $5,000. Those expenses have not yet been paid, so they will be recorded under accounts payable. These costs are also accounted for in inventories.

An increase in inventories is recorded as a debit. Accounts payable and depreciation are both credited because accounts payable is a liability, and depreciation reduces assets.

Debit		Credit	
Inventories	11,250	Depreciation	6,250
		Accounts Payable	5,000

Double Entry Activity 7: Book Depreciation and SG&A Expenses

Activity 7 recorded the depreciation of the office included in the SG&A expense of $2,000, other SG&A expenses of $5,000 as an advertising expenses (on credit) and your salary as CEO. The take-home pay was $26,250, and the company would eventually pay a $14,000 social security fee.

SG&A expenses are period expenses that directly affect the IS, and this increase in expenses is debited. The corresponding credit requires more than one entry, including the office depreciation of $2,000, accounts payable for advertising expenses of $5,000, the $26,250 cash payment of CEO salary, and accrued expenses for the unpaid payroll-related expenses of $14,000.

Debit		Credit	
SG&A Expenses	47,250	Cash	26,250
		Accounts Payable	5,000
		Accrued Expenses	14,000
		Depreciation	2,000

Double Entry Activity 9: Ship Products

In Activity 9, Showa Senbei sold 50,300 packages for $4 per package. The cost of goods sold was $2 per package, so an increase in sales of $201,200 (50,300

[複式簿記] **活動6：減価償却費と製造間接費を計上する**

活動6は製造間接費にあたる減価償却6,250ドルとその他光熱費など5,000ドルを計上しました。光熱費などはまだ支払っていないので仕入債務に計上します。また，これらの費用はいったん棚卸資産に計上されます。

棚卸資産が増えることは借方に仕訳されます。仕入債務は負債なので貸方に仕訳されます。そして減価償却費は資産を減少させるのでやはり貸方です。

借　方	貸　方
棚卸資産　　11,250	減価償却　　6,250 仕入債務　　5,000

[複式簿記] **活動7：減価償却費と販管費を計上する**

活動7は販管費である事務所の減価償却費2,000ドル，その他の販管費として販売促進費（掛けでの支払い）5,000ドルと，社長としてのあなたの給料を計上しました。給料の手取り金額は26,250ドル，それに伴う社会保険料などの会社がいずれ支払うコストは14,000ドルでした。

販管費は直接PLに影響を与える期間費用です。費用の増加は借方に仕訳されます。対応する貸方は複数の仕訳が必要です。事務所の減価償却費は2,000ドル，販売促進費分の仕入債務5,000ドル，社長の給与のうち，現金支払い分の26,250ドル，そして未払いの給与関連費用が未払費用で14,000ドルとなります。

借　方	貸　方
販管費　　47,250	現　　金　　26,250 仕入債務　　　5,000 未払費用　　14,000 減価償却　　　2,000

[複式簿記] **活動9：製品を出荷する**

活動9では，「昭和せんべい」は1袋あたり4ドルの価格で50,300袋を販売しました（掛け売り）。この分の売上原価は1袋あたり2ドルでした。売上の

packages×$4) is credited. Corresponding to this sales increase, accounts receivable is an asset, so it is debited. $100,600 (50,300 packages×$2) of inventory shipped is recorded as a cost and debited. The same amount of inventories is reduced and credited.

Debit		Credit	
Accounts Receivable	201,200	Sales	201,200
Cost of Goods Sold	100,600	Inventories	100,600

As shown in Figure 3.12, the double entry system creates the IS and BS by arranging journals. The profit deducting cost from sales in the IS is linked to the retained earnings of the BS, so the total assets and the total liabilities & shareholders' equity are balanced.

Figure 3.12 ▌ IS and BS Corresponding to Activity 9

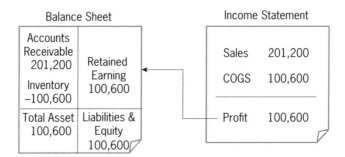

176 | Section 3 Double Entry System

増加 201,200 ドル（50,300 袋 × 4 ドル）は貸方に計上されます。これに対応する売上債権は資産ですので借方に仕訳されます。出荷した分の在庫 100,600 ドル（50,300 袋 × 2 ドル）は原価となり，費用の増加なので借方に仕訳されます。そしてこの分は棚卸資産の減額になり，貸方に仕訳されます。

借　　方		貸　　方	
売上債権	201,200	売 上 高	201,200
売上原価	100,600	棚卸資産	100,600

　さらに，図表 3.12 が示すように，複式簿記では仕訳の情報を組み替えることにより PL と BS を作成することができます。PL で売上高から売上原価を差し引いた利益が，BS の利益剰余金にリンクしており，BS の資産と負債・株主資本はバランスします。

図表 3.12 ┃ 活動 9 の PL と BS

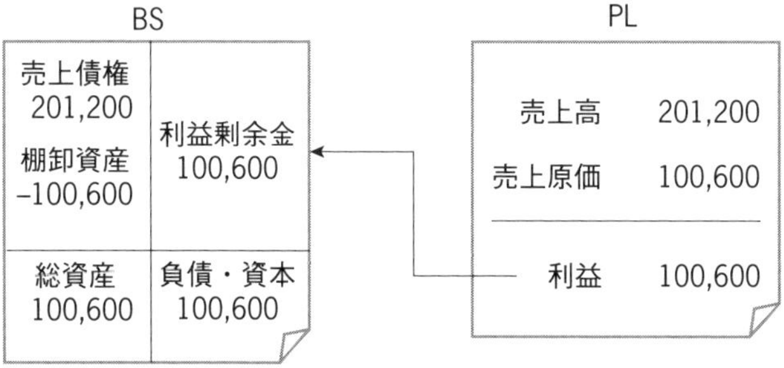

● Full Picture of Double Entry

We have explored the double entry system while looking back on some activities of Showa Senbei, but to understand the full picture of the double entry system, let us use another example of business.

In the activities below, let as assume this business sells purchased products as they are, such as a company operating in the retail industry, and journal the activities from ① to ⑧ .

① The company is established with a 7 million yen investment. The company increases assets in the form of cash, journaled as debit, and the capital stock of shareholders' equity increases, journaled as credit.

Debit	Credit
Cash 7,000,000	Capital Stock 7,000,000

② The company borrows 4 million yen from the bank. The cash is debited, and the debt is credited.

Debit	Credit
Cash 4,000,000	Debt 4,000,000

③ The company then purchases store-related equipment in cash for 6 million yen. This equipment is now one of the company's assets. Property, plant & equipment increases, so it is debited, while cash (an asset) decreases, so it is journaled as a credit.

Debit	Credit
PP&E 6,000,000	Cash 6,000,000

④ The company purchases the goods that will be sold for 4 million yen on credit. The inventories (subsection of assets) increases, which is journaled as a debit. Accounts payable increases (subsection of liabilities) and is journaled as a credit.

「昭和せんべい」のいくつかの活動を振り返りながら複式簿記の説明をしてきましたが，別の事業活動の例を使用して，複式簿記の全体像をとらえましょう。

ここでは小売業のように，仕入れた商品をそのまま販売するようなビジネスを想定します。①から⑧までの活動を仕訳していきましょう。

① 700万円出資して会社を設立します。会社としては現金という資産が増えるので借方に，株主資本の資本金が増えるので貸方に仕訳します。

借　方		貸　方	
現　金	7,000,000	資本金	7,000,000

② 400万円銀行から借り入れます。現金という資産が増えるので借方に，負債が増えるので貸方に仕訳します。

借　方		貸　方	
現　金	4,000,000	借入金	4,000,000

③ 600万円で店舗関連の備品を現金払いで購入します。この備品は固定資産です。固定資産が増えるので借方に，現金という資産が減るので貸方に仕訳します。

借　方		貸　方	
固定資産	6,000,000	現　金	6,000,000

④ 販売用の商品を掛けで400万円購入します。棚卸資産が増えるので借方に，買掛金という負債が増えるので貸方に仕訳します。

Debit		Credit	
Inventories	4,000,000	Accounts Payable	4,000,000

⑤ The company pays 2 million yen for labor costs. Labor costs in the retail industry are classified as SG&A expenses. SG&A expenses increase and are debited. Meanwhile, cash is paid, and assets are reduced, so it is entered into credits.

Debit		Credit	
SG&A Expenses	2,000,000	Cash	2,000,000

⑥ 1 million yen is paid for rent. Rent for a retail business can be regarded as SG&A expenses. SG&A expenses increase and are journaled as a debit. Meanwhile, cash is paid, and assets are reduced, so this is journaled as a credit.

Debit		Credit	
SG&A Expenses	1,000,000	Cash	1,000,000

⑦ The 1.2 million yen depreciation is recognized, which is regarded as an SG&A expense in retail businesses. Therefore, SG&A expenses increase which is journaled as a debit. Meanwhile, depreciation reduces the value of a PP&E, so it is credited.

Debit		Credit	
SG&A Expenses	1,200,000	PP&E	1,200,000

⑧ The company sells goods purchased during activity ④ for 9 million yen (selling on credit), so these sales are journaled as credits. Due to those sales, accounts receivable increases by the same amount, and is journaled as a debit. The decrease in inventories for the goods sold is entered as a credit, and correspondingly the cost of goods sold is debited by the same amount.

Debit		Credit	
Accounts Receivable	9,000,000	Sales	9,000,000
Cost of Goods Sold	4,000,000	Inventories	4,000,000

借　方	貸　方
棚卸資産　　4,000,000	買 掛 金　　4,000,000

⑤　人件費を 200 万円支払います。小売業の人件費は販管費です。販管費は費用なので借方に，現金を支払い資産が減るので貸方に仕訳します。

借　方	貸　方
販 管 費　　2,000,000	現　　金　　2,000,000

⑥　賃貸料 100 万円支払います。小売業の賃貸料は販管費と考えていいでしょう。販管費は費用なので借方に，現金を支払い資産が減るので貸方に仕訳します。

借　方	貸　方
販 管 費　　1,000,000	現　　金　　1,000,000

⑦　減価償却費 120 万円を計上します。小売業の減価償却費は販管費と考えていいでしょう。販管費は費用なので借方に仕訳します。減価償却は資産の価値を減額するものなので資産が減少し，貸方に仕訳します。

借　方	貸　方
販 管 費　　1,200,000	固定資産　　1,200,000

⑧　④で購入した商品を 900 万円で販売（掛け売り）します。売上は貸方に仕訳し，それに対応して発生する売掛金は資産なので借方に仕訳します。販売した分の棚卸資産の減少は貸方に仕訳され，それが売上原価という費用になるので借方に仕訳します。

借　方	貸　方
売 掛 金　　9,000,000	売 上 高　　9,000,000
売上原価　　4,000,000	棚卸資産　　4,000,000

Debit and credit match all the time. The results of the journal so far are summarized in Figure 3.13.

Figure 3.13 | All Journals (in yen)

		Debit		Credit	
①	Incorporate a company investing 7,000,000	Cash	7,000,000	Capital Stock	7,000,000
②	Borrow 4,000,000	Cash	4,000,000	Debt	4,000,000
③	Purchase store equipment, paying 6,000,000	PP&E	6,000,000	Cash	6,000,000
④	Purchase goods to be sold worth 4,000,000 on credit	Inventory	4,000,000	Accounts Payable	4,000,000
⑤	Pay salary to workers of 2,000,000	SG&A	2,000,000	Cash	2,000,000
⑥	Pay rent of 1,000,000	SG&A	1,000,000	Cash	1,000,000
⑦	Book depreciation of 1,200,000	SG&A (Depreciation)	1,200,000	PP&E	1,200,000
⑧	Sell all goods purchased in ④ totalling 9,000,000 on credit	Accounts Receivable	9,000,000	Sales	9,000,000
		COGS	4,000,000	Inventory	4,000,000

● Trial Balance

Next, the journaled data is summed by accounting item and organized on the side where it is entered positively. Items categorized into assets and expenses are summarized as debit, and items categorized into liabilities, shareholders' equity, and sales are summarized as credit. For example, the cash balance should be 7 million in ① , plus 4 million in ② , minus 6 million in ③ , minus 2 million in ⑤ , and minus 1 million in ⑥ , totaling 2 million yen.

Tables organized in this way are called **trial balances** (Figure 3.14).

いずれも借方と貸方の額が一致します。ここまでの仕訳の結果を図表 3.13
にまとめています。

図表 3.13 ┃ 仕訳の全体像

		借 方		貸 方	
①	700 万円出資して会社を設立する	現　　金	7,000,000	資 本 金	7,000,000
②	400 万円銀行から借入れ	現　　金	4,000,000	借 入 金	4,000,000
③	600 万円で店舗関連の備品を購入	固定資産	6,000,000	現　　金	6,000,000
④	商品を掛けで 400 万円購入	棚卸資産	4,000,000	買 掛 金	4,000,000
⑤	人件費を 200 万円支払う	販 管 費	2,000,000	現　　金	2,000,000
⑥	賃貸料 100 万円支払う	販 管 費	1,000,000	現　　金	1,000,000
⑦	減価償却費 120 万円計上	販管費（減価償却費）	1,200,000	固定資産	1,200,000
⑧	④で購入した商品を 900 万円で販売（掛け売り）	売 掛 金 売上原価	9,000,000 4,000,000	売 上 高 棚卸資産	9,000,000 4,000,000

● 残高試算表

次に，仕訳されたデータは，項目別にプラスで仕訳される側に合計されて整
理されます。資産と費用の項目は借方に，負債と株主資本と売上の項目は貸方
で合計されるということです。たとえば現金であれば，①でプラス 700 万円，
②でプラス 400 万円，③でマイナス 600 万円，⑤でマイナス 200 万円，⑥でマ
イナス 100 万円の合計で残高は 200 万円となります。

このように整理された表は**残高試算表**と呼ばれます（図表 3.14）。

Figure 3.14 | Trial Balance

Debit		Credit	
Cash	2,000,000	Accounts Payable	4,000,000
Accounts Receivable	9,000,000	Debt	4,000,000
Inventory	0	Capital Stock	7,000,000
PP&E	4,800,000		
COGS	4,000,000	Sales	9,000,000
SG&A	4,200,000		

● Prepare Balance Sheet and Income Statement

The trial balance aggregates the results of all activities. Please note that the trial balance looks similar to the BS.

You can create an IS and BS by cutting the trial balance up or down. As shown in Figure 3.15, the IS is prepared by subtracting COGS and SG&A from Sales to derive the income, and when the income is linked with retained earnings, the left and right of the BS become balanced.

Figure 3.15 | Prepare BS and IS from the Trial Balance

Balance Sheet			
Cash	2,000,000	Accounts Receivable	4,000,000
Accounts Payable	9,000,000	Debt	4,000,000
Inventory	0	Capital Stock	7,000,000
PP&E	4,800,000	Retained Earnings	800,000
Total Asset	15,800,000	Total Liabilities & Equity	15,800,000

Income Statement			
COGS	4,000,000	Sales	9,000,000
SG&A	4,200,000		
Income	800,000		

借　方		貸　方	
現　　金	2,000,000	買掛金	4,000,000
売 掛 金	9,000,000	借入金	4,000,000
棚卸資産	0	資本金	7,000,000
固定資産	4,800,000		
売上原価	4,000,000	売上高	9,000,000
販 管 費	4,200,000		

❶ BS, PL の作成

　残高試算表にはすべての活動の結果が集約されています。そして，この表が BS に似ていることもわかるでしょう。

　実は，残高試算表を上下に切り離すと，PL と BS が作成できます。図表 3.15 のように，売上から売上原価と販管費を引いて利益を算出すれば PL になりますし，利益の額を BS の利益剰余金にリンクさせれば，BS はきっちり左右がバランスするのです。

図表 3.15 ┃ 残高試算表から BS, PL の作成

貸借対照表

現　　金	2,000,000	買 掛 金	4,000,000
売 掛 金	9,000,000	借 入 金	4,000,000
棚卸資産	0	資 本 金	7,000,000
固定資産	4,800,000	利益剰余金	800,000
総 資 産	15,800,000	負債及び純資産	15,800,000

損益計算書

売上原価	4,000,000	売 上 高	9,000,000
販 管 費	4,200,000		
利　　益	800,000		

● Prepare Cash Flow Statement

The BS and IS are composed. but how does the double entry system prepare cash flow statements? Remember the discussion in the previous section. CFS can be prepared based on the data in the IS and the BS (Figure 3.16).

Figure 3.16 ❙ **Prepare a Cash Flow Statement from the IS and BS**

	Income	800,000
+	Depreciation	1,200,000
−	Increase in Accounts Receivable	9,000,000
−	Increase in Inventory	0
+	Increase in Accounts Payable	4,000,000
	Cash Flow from Operation	−3,000,000
	Capital Expenditure	−6,000,000
	Cash Flow from Investment	−6,000,000
	Share Issurance	7,000,000
+	Increase in Debt	4,000,000
	Cash Flow from Financing	11,000,000
	Change in Cash	2,000,000
+	Beginning Cash Balance	0
=	Ending Cash Balance	2,000,000

BS, PL はできましたが, 複式簿記ではキャッシュフロー計算書はどのように作られるのでしょうか。これは前のセクションで紹介した通りです。キャッシュフロー計算書は PL と BS のデータに基づいて作成できます（図表 3.16）。

図表 3.16 ▎ **PL, BS からのキャッシュフロー計算書の作成**

	利益	800,000
＋	減価償却費	1,200,000
－	売掛金増	9,000,000
－	棚卸資産増	0
＋	買掛金増	4,000,000
営業 CF		−3,000,000
	固定資産取得	−6,000,000
投資 CF		−6,000,000
	株式発行	7,000,000
＋	借入金増	4,000,000
財務 CF		11,000,000
現金増減額		2,000,000
＋	期首現金残高	0
＝	期末現金残高	2,000,000

● Effectiveness of Double Entry System

A double entry system is extremely effective for accurately recording the economic value of business activities and is essential for accounting. Financial accounting organizes, reports, and analyzes information recorded through the double entry system. Furthermore, it is not necessary to understand how business activities affect each of the three financial statements as we discussed in Chapter 2 to master the double entry system.

The great thing about the double entry system is that if you correctly journal business activities according to the five classifications: assets, liabilities, shareholders' equity, expenses, and sales, then the IS and BS are automatically constructed by totaling each item under debit and credit.

Therefore, it is easy to create financial statements if you understand or remember the minimum rules of the double entry system; debiting if assets and expenses increase, and crediting if liabilities, shareholders' equity, and sales increase.

● 複式簿記の有効性

　複式簿記は事業活動の経済的価値を正確に記録するために極めて有効であり，会計に欠かすことはできません。財務会計は複式簿記により記録された情報を整理し，報告し，分析していきます。実は簿記を学ぶ際には，第2章で議論したような事業活動が財務三表にそれぞれどう影響するのかを1つひとつ理解する必要はありません。

　複式簿記のすごいところは，事業活動を資産，負債，株主資本，費用，売上という会計項目の5分類にしたがって正しく仕訳しさえすれば，借方と貸方の数値を合算することで，自動的にPLとBSが作成されてしまうことにあります。

　そのため，資産と費用が増えれば借方に仕訳し，負債と株主資本と売上が増えれば貸方に仕訳する，という複式簿記の最低限のルールを理解，あるいは覚えさえすれば，財務諸表を作成することは容易に可能なのです。

Section 4 Accounting Standards

○ Accounting with Dialects

As stated at the beginning, accounting is a common language throughout the whole world of business. Therefore, accounting information must be handled following standardized rules. Otherwise, you would face great differences in interpreting financial information.

However, accounting is like a language with a local dialect. Depending on the country's background, culture, and the history of industrial development, accounting standards may vary.

To unify these, the International Financial Reporting Standards (**IFRS**) set common rules to ensure that financial statements are consistently transparent and comparable around the world.

IFRS is used in more than 140 countries, but the United States and Japan are examples of two counties whose financial reporting standards differ slightly from the IFRS.

○ Generally Accepted Accounting Principles (GAAP)

The accounting rules that each country adopts in principle are referred to as the "Generally Accepted Accounting Principles" or "**GAAP**".

A public company listed in the U.S. is required to comply with the standards (USGAAP) issued by the U.S. Financial Accounting Standards Board, or FASB. A company listed in Japan generally follows Japanese accounting standards (also known as JGAAP), but can also report by IFRS, and USGAAP standards if the company is listed in the U. S.

The following are some examples of the differences in reported figures based on these different accounting standards.

第4節 会計基準

方言のある会計

　冒頭でも説明しましたが，会計はビジネスを行う上での全世界における共通言語です。そのため，会計情報は基本的に標準化されたルールに則って取り扱う必要があります。さもなければ，財務情報の解釈に違いが出てきてしまうからです。

　しかしながら，会計は地域によって方言がある言語ともいえます。その地域の文化や産業発展の歴史といった背景の違いによって，会計基準は国や地域によって若干異なるのです。

　これらを統一するために，国際財務報告基準（IFRS）は，財務諸表が一貫して透明性を保ち，世界中で比較可能になるように，共通のルールを設定しています。

　IFRS は 140 カ国以上で使用されています。ところが，全面的に使用する国の中に米国および日本は含まれていないのです。

一般に公正妥当と認められた会計基準（GAAP）

　各国が原則として認める会計処理に関するルールのことを「一般に公正妥当と認められた会計基準（GAAP）」と呼びます。

　米国の上場企業は，米国財務会計基準審議会（FASB）が発行した基準（USGAAP）に従う必要があります。また，日本の上場企業は一般的に日本の会計基準（JGAAP とも呼ばれる）に従いますが，IFRS に準じた報告を行うこととともでき，また米国に上場している場合は USGAAP に準じた報告を行うこともできます。

　以下では，会計基準が異なると報告数値が異なってくる例をいくつか示します。

As seen in Showa Senbei, the cost of manufacturing products is recorded in inventories, then entered into the cost of goods sold at the time of sale. There are multiple ways to calculate the value of inventory and COGS.

They include the **first-in, first-out method (FIFO)** based on the idea of being sold sequentially starting with the oldest (first) inventory, the **last-in, first-out method (LIFO)** based on the idea of being sold sequentially starting from the newest (last) inventory, and the **average method** that assigns the average cost of all the company's inventory.

Each of these three methods frequently account for different numbers when constructing the IS and BS (but cash flow will always remain unchanged).

Figure 3.17 demonstrates a simple numerical example of how numbers are recorded in the IS and BS based on each method, even if it is the same business activities.

Let us assume that we are a retail or wholesale business entity that purchases and sells some goods to customers. First, the entity purchases 100 pieces of goods for $10 per piece, resulting in the inventory value of $1,000 (=$10×100 pieces.) Next, the entity purchases another 100 pieces of the same goods for $15 per piece, increasing the inventory value by $1,500 (=$15×100 pieces.) After the first and second purchases, the total inventory is valued at $2,500 for 200 pieces.

Then, the entity sells 100 pieces of goods. If the sales price is $20 per piece, sales revenue is $2,000. What about the cost of goods sold corresponding to the sales?

● 在庫の評価方法の違い

　「昭和せんべい」の例でみたように，商品製造にかかわるコストはいったん棚卸資産（在庫）に計上され，販売された段階で売上原価に計上されます。実は，この在庫の価値および原価への計上額を計算する方法は複数あります。

　古い（最初の）在庫から順番に販売されるという考え方に基づく「**先入れ先出し法**」（FIFO），新しい（最後の）在庫から順番に販売されるという考え方に基づく「**後入れ先出し法**」（LIFO），およびすべての在庫の平均を使用する「**平均法**」です。

　これらの 3 つの方法は，多くの場合，損益計算書および貸借対照表において異なる数値を計上します（なお，キャッシュフローはどのような方法をとろうとも変わりません）。

　図表 3.17 は全く同じ事業活動だとしても，それぞれの方法によってどのような数値が PL と BS に記録されるのかを簡単な数値例で示したものです。

　ここでは，商品を仕入れて販売する小売・卸業のようなビジネスを想定します。まず，この商品を 1 個あたり 10 ドルで 100 個仕入れます。在庫（棚卸資産）の価値は 10 ドル× 100 個なので 1,000 ドルになります。次に同じ商品を 1 個 15 ドルでやはり 100 個仕入れたとします。在庫の価値は 15 ドル× 100 個で 1,500 ドル増加します。1 回目の仕入れと 2 回目の仕入れ全体では，商品を 200 個仕入れ，在庫の価値は 2,500 ドルとなります。

　このうち，100 個商品を販売したとしましょう。仮に 1 個あたり 20 ドルで販売すれば，売上高は 2,000 ドルです。ではこの売上高に対応する売上原価はどうなるでしょうか。

Figure 3.17 | Inventory Valuation and the Impact on IS and BS

Purchase	Units	Price	Inventory Value			FIFO	LIFO	Average
1	100	$10.00	$1,000	Sales		$2,000	$2,000	$2,000
2	100	$15.00	$1,500	Cost of Goods Sold		$1,000	$1,500	$1,250
Total	200		$2,500	Profit		$1,000	$500	$750

Selling	Units	Price	Sales	Ending		$1,500	$1,000	$1,250
	100	$20.00	$2,000	Inventory				

FIFO assumes that the 100 pieces purchased earlier are sold first, so the cost of goods sold is recorded at $1,000, and the balance of inventory on the BS after the sale is $1,500.

On the other hand, LIFO assumes that 100 pieces purchased later are sold first, so the cost of goods sold is recorded as $1,500, and the balance of inventory on the BS after the sale is $1,000.

Lastly, the average method calculated the average inventory value of goods to be $12.5 per piece, which is derived by dividing the total inventory value of $2,500 by the total inventory amount of 200 pieces. So $1,250 which is the product of the average value of $12.5 multiplied by 100 pieces, is recorded as the cost of goods sold. After the sale, the remaining balance of inventory on the BS is also $1,250.

Different inventory valuation methods calculate different costs of goods sold, naturally creating different profits in the IS ($1,000 with FIFO, $500 with LIFO, and $750 with the average method), and different figures in the BS. Various financial measures such as ROA will change, because of these different values.

USGAAP allows LIFO, while JGAAP and IFRS do not. Therefore, companies complying with JGAAP and IFRS use FIFO or the average method for inventory valuation.

図表 3.17 ┃ 在庫の評価方法と PL，BS への影響

仕入れ	個数	価格	棚卸資産			FIFO	LIFO	平均法
1	100	$10.00	$1,000	売上高		$2,000	$2,000	$2,000
2	100	$15.00	$1,500	売上原価		$1,000	$1,500	$1,250
合計	200		$2,500	利益		$1,000	$500	$750
販売	個数	価格	売上高	期末棚卸		$1,500	$1,000	$1,250
	100	$20.00	$2,000	資産残高				

先入れ先出し法では，先に仕入れた 100 個の商品を売ったと想定するので，売上原価は 1,000 ドルとなり，販売後の貸借対照表上の在庫の残高は 1,500 ドルになります。

一方で，後入れ先出し法では，後に仕入れた 100 個の商品を売ったと想定するので，売上原価は 1,500 ドルになり，販売後の貸借対照表上の在庫の残高は 1,000 ドルになります。

さらに平均法では，まず全体の在庫の価値 2,500 ドルを 200 個で割った商品 1 個あたりの平均的な在庫の価値 12.5 ドルを計算します。そしてこの 12.5 ドルに 100 個を掛けた 1,250 ドルが売上原価となり，販売後の貸借対照表上の在庫の残高も 1,250 ドルとなります。

異なる在庫の評価方法を用いることにより，売上原価が変化するので，当然ながら損益計算書上の利益も変わり（先入れ先出し法だと 1,000 ドル，後入れ先出し法だと 500 ドル，平均法だと 750 ドル），また貸借対照表の数値も変わります。結果として ROA などの財務指標も変化することになります。

USGAAP では，後入れ先出し法による計算は認められていますが，IFRS および日本の会計基準では後入れ先出し法は認められていません。そのため IFRS および日本の会計基準を使用する企業では，在庫の評価は先入れ先出し法あるいは平均法を用いて計算することになります。

○ Difference in Treatment of Goodwill

When a company acquires another company, the assets of the acquired company are recorded at fair value on the BS of the acquiring company. In most cases, the acquisition price is different from the fair value, and usually exceeds the fair value reflecting the prospect of the acquired company. The difference between the acquisition price and the fair value is called **goodwill** (Figure 3.18).

Figure 3.18 | Goodwill

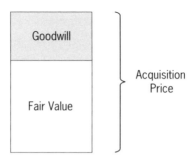

Goodwill is considered to represent the value of a variety of invisible assets including brand, technical capabilities, sales channels, customer base, and human resources held by the acquired company, and is recorded as an intangible asset on the BS of the acquiring company.

Under JGAAP, goodwill is amortized (same meaning as depreciated) similarly to treating tangible fixed assets and are equally expensed within 20 years. For example, if goodwill is initially recorded for 2 billion yen and is amortized over 10 years, annual amortization of 200 million yen will be recorded as expenses in the IS, and the balance of goodwill on the BS will decrease by that amount.

Meanwhile, under IFRS and USGAAP, goodwill is not amortized in principle, and expensed only if the value of goodwill is significantly impaired based on the annual valuation. (This treatment is called "write off" or "impairment".) Companies that apply IFRS or USGAAP tend to have larger profits in normal states because they do not have to incur goodwill amortization.

◉ のれんの取り扱いにおける違い

　企業が他の企業を買収するとき，買収される（被買収）企業の資産は，買収する企業の貸借対照表上に公正な価値で計上されます。企業を買収する場合に支払われる買収金額は，公正価値とは異なるケースがほとんどであり，通常は被買収企業の将来性を反映して，買収金額は資産の公正価値を上回ります。この買収金額と公正価値の差額が「**のれん**」です（図表 3.18）。

図表 3.18 ┃ のれん

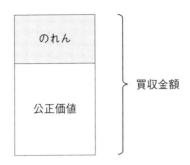

　のれんは被買収企業のブランドや技術力，販売チャネルや顧客基盤，人的資源などを含むさまざまな見えない資産価値を表わしていると考えられ，無形固定資産として，買収する企業の貸借対照表に計上されます。

　日本の会計基準では，のれんは有形固定資産の取り扱いと同じように減価償却費を計上していき，20 年以内の期間で均等に償却されます。たとえば，のれんが 20 億円あるとして，10 年間で償却する場合，毎年 2 億円の償却費が費用として損益計算書に計上され，貸借対照表ののれんの残高はその分減っていくことになります。

　一方で，IFRS と USGAAP では，原則としてのれんの償却は行わず，毎年行われる評価結果に基づいて，著しくのれんの価値が損なわれたと判断された場合にのみ，費用として計上します（このことを減損処理といいます）。IFRS や USGAAP を適用する会社のほうが，のれん償却がない分，通常時の利益は多くなりがちです。

Section

5 Accounting's Limitations

● Behavior of Accounting

Chapter 1 stated that accounting shows various business activities as monetary value. Therefore, events that cannot be measured financially are not recorded, even if they are very important. Besides, accounting basically deals with only past events, so events that may occur in the future are not considered in accounting. Accounting only records history.

● Market Value and Book Value

The BS in the accounting framework is based on its acquisition price. For example, the value of PP&E is shown as the acquisition price minus the cumulative value of depreciation. The value of finished goods inventory is recorded based on the manufacturing costs. Such value on the book is called book value.

However, book value is often different from the market value which is the value of the company if it is currently trading. For example, the market value of equipment for manufacturing special tools would decline significantly if the tools become obsolete. In this case, the book value of the equipment is higher than the market value. On the other hand, land purchased decades ago can be recorded on BS at a much lower price than the current market value (market value > book value).

● Market Value of a Company

How is the market value decided? Since the following is a topic of finance rather than accounting, it is not discussed in detail in this book. Please refer to a finance textbook if you are interested further.

The market value of an asset is based on the present value of the cash flow that the

第5節 会計の限界

会計の性質

　第1章において，会計はさまざまな事業活動を金銭的な価値として示すことを述べました。そのため金銭的に測定が不可能な出来事は，それがたとえ非常に重要であったとしても記録されません。また，会計が記録するのは基本的に過去の出来事に限られます。将来発生する可能性のある出来事は会計ではとらえられません。会計は歴史を記録するものだからです。

時価と簿価

　会計の枠組みにおける貸借対照表は，その取得価格をベースに示されています。たとえば固定資産の価値であれば取得価格から減価償却費の累計額を引いた額として表わされます。また製品の棚卸資産であれば，その製品の製造にかかったコストによって価値は計上されます。このような帳簿上の価値は簿価と呼ばれます。

　しかし，簿価は現在それが取引されたらいくらなのかという市場価値（時価）とは多くの場合異なります。たとえば，特殊な道具を製造するための設備の市場価値は，その道具が使われなくなったとしたら大きく下がるでしょう。この場合の設備の簿価は時価よりも高いものとなります。一方で，数十年前に購入された土地は現在の市場価値よりもはるかに低い価格で貸借対照表に計上されているでしょう（時価＞簿価）。

企業の市場価値

　時価である市場価値はどのように決まるのでしょうか。以下は会計というよりもファイナンスのトピックですので，本書では詳しく議論しません。興味のある方はファイナンス関連の書籍を参照ください。

　資産の市場価値は，その資産が将来にわたって生み出すキャッシュフローの

asset will generate in the future. When it is applied to a company, the market value of the company is decided by;

"the present value of the cash flows the company will generate in the future".

Figure 3.19 | Value of Company

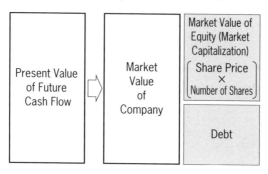

The value of a company is comprised of two components: the value of debt and the value of shareholders' equity. The market value of shareholders' equity is also called the market capitalization and is calculated as the current share price multiplied by the number of shares. The value of a company is determined by cash flows generated by the company in the future. The stream of cash flow can be divided into those attributed to creditors and banks (debt holders) and those attributed to equity shareholders.

◉ Can Accounting Explain Corporate Value?

Cash flow attributable to creditors and banks is a payment of interest and repayment of principal for a company. This cash flow is stable because it is decided upon a contract, so the value of the debt does not diverge from the book value unless the company faces an extreme event, such as being threatened by bankruptcy.

On the other hand, cash flow attributable to shareholders is the residual cash flow after subtracting the cash flow to the creditors from the total cash flow of the company. Therefore, cash flow attributable to shareholders is not stable and the value

現在価値によって決まります。これを企業に当てはめると，企業の市場価値は「その企業が将来にわたって生み出すキャッシュフローの現在価値」によって決まるということです。

図表 3.19 ┃ 企業価値

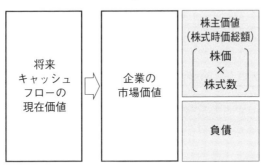

企業価値は大きく負債の価値と，株式つまり株主資本の価値に分けられます。なお，株主資本の時価は株式時価総額とも呼ばれ，その時点の株価と株数を掛け合わせたものです。企業価値は企業が将来にわたって生み出すキャッシュフローによって決まるのですが，そのキャッシュフローが債権者や銀行に帰属するものと，株主に帰属するものとに分けられるということです。

❍ 会計は企業価値を説明できるのか

債権者・銀行に帰属するキャッシュフローは企業にとってみると利息の支払いと元本の返済です。このキャッシュフローは契約によって前もって決まっていますから安定しており，負債の価値というのはよほどでない限り（企業が倒産の危機に瀕しない限り）簿価から乖離しません。

一方，株主に帰属するキャッシュフローは，企業が生み出したキャッシュフローから，負債に帰属するキャッシュフローを差し引いた残りです。そのため，株主に帰属するキャッシュフローは安定せず，株主資本の価値は企業の将来の

of shareholders' equity varies significantly depending on the company's future cash flow outlook. As a result, the stock price of listed companies fluctuates every day.

So how much is the difference between the book value of equity on the balance sheet, or shareholders' equity in the accounting framework, and the market capitalization or the market value of equity? Figure 3.20 compares the market capitalization of representative U.S. companies with the shareholders' equity from the balance sheet.

Figure 3.20 ┃ Shareholders' Equity and Market Capitalization

Fiscal Year Ending	Amazon Dec-19	Apple Sep-20	Microsoft Jun-20	Tesla Dec-19	Coca-Cola Dec-19
Shareholders' Equity	62,060	65,339	118,304	6,618	18,981
Market Capitalization	1,587,000	2,078,000	1,621,000	567,831	231,417

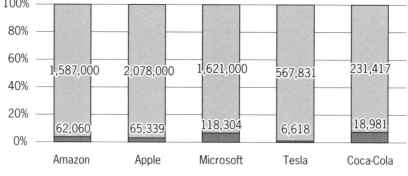

(Millions of dollars, market capitalization as of December 2020)

Accounting shareholders' equity accounts for only a few percent of market capitalization. While accounting figures represent past financial conditions and performance, it is not rare that it only explains less than one-tenth of the market value of a company determined by its future expectations.

Why does this gap occur? Because a company's value is driven by the cash flow it

キャッシュフローの見通しにより大きく変動します。結果として，株式市場で取引されている上場会社の株価は日々変動するのです。

　では，会計の枠組みによる貸借対照表上の株主資本，つまり株主資本の簿価は，株式時価総額とどれだけの差があるのでしょうか。図表 3.20 は代表的な米国企業の株式時価総額と貸借対照表上の株主資本の額を比較したものです。

図表 3.20 ▌ 株主資本と時価総額

決算期	アマゾン 2019 年 12 月	アップル 2020 年 9 月	マイクロソフト 2020 年 6 月	テスラ 2019 年 12 月	コカ・コーラ 2019 年 12 月
株主資本	62,060	65,339	118,304	6,618	18,981
株式時価総額	1,587,000	2,078,000	1,621,000	567,831	231,417

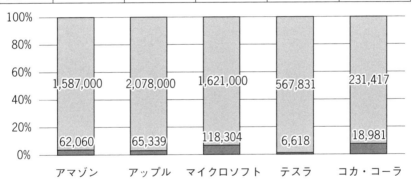

■株主資本　□株式時価総額

（単位：百万ドル，時価総額は 2020 年 12 月時点）

　会計上の株主資本は時価総額の数％にとどまっています。このように，会計上の数値というのは過去の財務状態や業績を表わしているものの，将来期待に基づく企業価値に関しては 10 分の 1 も説明できないことは珍しくありません。

　このギャップはどうして生じるのでしょうか。企業の価値はその企業が生み

generates. All of its competitive advantages including its business models, such as customer satisfaction, loyalty, brand, product development capabilities, efficient manufacturing and supply chains, financing flexibilities, the leadership of top management, capable employees, and organizational structure to make a decision swiftly, can be factors for the gap.

Accounting is an essential knowledge of business. However, extensive knowledge of marketing, R&D, technology, engineering, finance, logistics, human resource management, etc. are also essential to increase the value of a company.

出すキャッシュフローによって決まるのですから，顧客満足度やロイヤリティー，ブランド，商品開発力，効率的な製造工程やサプライチェーン，資金調達の柔軟性，経営者のリーダーシップ，従業員の能力，迅速な意思決定ができる経営体制など企業のビジネスモデルを含む競争優位性のすべてがこのギャップの要因となります。

　会計はビジネスにおける必須の知識です。しかしながら，企業の価値を高めるためには，マーケティング，研究開発，テクノロジー，エンジニアリング，ファイナンス，ロジスティック，人的資源管理，等にかかわる広範な知識もまた重要なのです。

Postface and Acknowledgement

I began teaching Financial Accounting in the 2020 (January-April) spring semester at Temple University, but the semester was interrupted by the novel coronavirus outbreak. The University decided to move all courses online on Friday, February 28, just in the middle of the semester, and after only a weekend of preparation, from the following Monday, March 2 we switched to online completely. Although teachers and students were unfamiliar with Zoom until then, the vocation to never stop teaching and learning made it possible to transfer classes online in a very short period of time. I was in the midst of that confusion, and witnessing everyone's reaction was indeed impressive.

Online classes demand more elaborate preparation to engage students and to supplement their learning. It was fortunate that I took advantage of the situation by utilizing the abundance of time at home that the state of emergency provided to write a new textbook.

This is the third book (the fourth including the second edition) to experience ascetic writing in this Japanese-English bilingual format. I struggled to write this book the most because the topic of financial accounting complies with the rules of accounting standards. For example, "net worth", "shareholders' equity" and "equity capital" on the balance sheet have essentially the same meaning, but under Japanese rules, these are slightly different. Additionally another concept that is beyond the contents of this book is how the Japanese and the U.S. starndards separate the invested capital by shareholders into "capital stock" and "additional paid-in capital" (Professor Robert C. Higgins at the University of Washington states in his book "Unless forced to do otherwise, my advice is to forget these distinctions. They keep accountants and attorneys employed, but seldom make much practical difference" (*Analysis for Financial Management 12th edition. McGraw-Hill, Page 12*)).

This distinction is unnecessary knowledge for ordinary business people, and only

あ と が き と 謝 辞

　私が Financial Accounting をテンプル大学で担当し始めた 2020 年の春学期（米国大学は 1 − 4 月）は新型コロナウイルス感染症の流行が始まった時期でもありました。テンプル大学ではちょうど学期の真ん中にあたる 2 月 28 日の金曜日にすべての講義をオンラインに変更することを決定し，週末の準備を経て翌月曜日の 3 月 2 日から全面的にオンライン講義に切り替えました。それまで Zoom の存在も知らなかった教員と学生たちが，絶対に教育・学びを止めないという使命感で超短期間でのオンライン化を可能にしたのです。私自身もその大混乱の真っただ中にいたわけですが，これには感動を覚えました。

　対面ではないクラスでは，有効な学習ツールを前提とした周到な講義の準備がさらに重要となります。緊急事態宣言の中でふんだんにとれた自宅での作業時間をあらたな教科書の執筆にあてられたことは，幸運なことでもありました。

　さて，私の日英対訳形式での書籍もこれで 3 冊目（第 2 版を含めると 4 冊目）となりました。どの本も大変でしたが，特に今回の財務会計というトピックは会計基準というルールに準拠しているため，いつにもまして執筆に苦労しました。たとえば，貸借対照表上の「純資産」と「株主資本」と「自己資本」は，本質的に意味合いは同じなのですが，厳密にいうと日本のルールにおいては若干異なっています。また，本書では触れていないトピックの 1 つとして，日本でも米国でも株主から出資された額は「資本金」と「資本準備金」とに分けて記載することになっていることがあります（ワシントン大学のロバート・C・ヒギンズ教授は著書の中で「どうしても必要なとき以外は，これらの区別を気にかけなくてもよい。これらは会計士と弁護士に仕事を与えているが，多くの場合実質的な違いはほとんどない」と述べています（『ファイナンシャル・マネジメント：企業財務の理論と実践（改訂 3 版）』グロービス経営大学院訳，ダイヤモンド社，13 ページ））。
　このような区別は普通のビジネスパーソンにとっては“全く必要ない”

complicates the discussion in many cases, but it is typically included as necessary information in a textbook that specifically caters to financial accounting. (I didn't include this information after all, though.)

In the meantime, there were new discoveries by organizing accounting items side by side in both languages. In Japanese, accounts receivable and accounts payable are expressed as a result of the action of selling or buying such as "the sales amount on credit" and "the purchase amount on credit". On the other hand in English, accounts receivable and accounts payable is expressed assuming future actions such as "the accounts to be received", and "the accounts to be paid". As of right now, I am not aware of the reason or background, but it was interesting to think if these different names were the result of a cultural difference. (Please let me know!)

I would like to thank the dedicated editors at Chuo-Keizai, Ms. Ayumi Sakai who read the text carefully. I am deeply grateful to students, colleagues, and everyone who encourages me all the time. For the completion of the book, the Research Assistant Grant Program provided by Temple University and support provided by Trevor Himstead, a teaching assistant there, was very helpful.

Lastly, in April 2021, I started teaching as a full-time faculty at Showa Women's University, which has a solid partnership with Temple University. In the meantime, I continue to serve as a Distinguished Scholar at Temple University and contribute to the development of the two universities flourishing collaborative relationship. I would like to express my deepest gratitude to all involved in both schools for providing the new challenge.

Spring to Summer, 2021

Akashi Hongo

知識であり，大体において議論を複雑にするだけなのですが，財務会計の教科書としては含めるべきなのかもしれないからです（結局これらは含めませんでしたが）。

　一方で，両言語で会計項目を横に並べて整理することで新たな発見もありました。日本語では売掛金・買掛金を，売った・買ったという行為の結果として，「掛けで売った金額」なので売掛金，「掛けで買った金額」なので買掛金と表現します。これに対し，英語では今後受け取る勘定，今後支払う勘定というように将来の行為を想定して表現しています。この違いにどんな理由や背景があるのかはわかりませんが，なんとなく名称の付け方にも文化的な違いがあるのかなと思いをはせることは興味深いものでした。（詳細ご存じであればお教えください）。

　前書から引き続きご担当いただいた中央経済社の阪井あゆみ様には丁寧に原稿に目を通していただきました。お礼申し上げます。また，学生，同僚をはじめとして，いつも刺激を与えてくれるすべての方々に深く感謝いたします。なお，本書の完成にあたってはテンプル大学内の Research Assistant Grant Program を活用し，学生であるトレヴァー・ヒムステッドのアシストを得ています。

　最後に私事ですが，2021 年 4 月から，テンプル大学と提携関係にあった昭和女子大学に常勤教員として所属し，またテンプル大学でも特別招聘教授として引き続き両校の協働による発展に貢献させていただくことになりました。新たなチャレンジの機会を用意していただいた両校の関係者の皆様にあらためて深くお礼申し上げます。

2021 年　春から夏

本合暁詩

Index／索引

About the Author

Akashi Hongo

Dr. Hongo is a Professor at Showa Women's University (SWU) and a Distinguished Scholar at Temple University, Japan Campus (TUJ). Prior to joining SWU and TUJ, Dr. Hongo was in charge of planning, accounting, human resource, legal, compliance, general affairs, international business development and supply chain management as a corporate officer at Recruit Management Solutions Co., Ltd. Dr. Hongo started his business career at Nippon Steel Co., Ltd. Then, he led value-based consulting practice in Japan and served as country representative for Stern Stewart & Co., a global consulting firm focusing on corporate finance and innovating the EVA framework. Dr. Hongo is the author of many books (in Japanese) on finance and management, including a bi-lingual (J-E) guide to corporate finance and valuation. He holds a BA from Keio University, an MBA from the International University of Japan, and a Ph.D from the International Christian University.

著者略歴

本合　暁詩

昭和女子大学グローバルビジネス学部ビジネスデザイン学科教授
テンプル大学ジャパンキャンパス特別招聘教授

新日本製鐵（現日本製鉄），スターン スチュワート日本支社長，リクルートマネジメントソ
リューションズ執行役員等を経て現職。経営指標 EVA®の導入コンサルティング，企業財務
分野での企業内研修講師，研究活動に加え，事業会社における経営管理業務全般を経験。
慶應義塾大学法学部卒業，国際大学大学院国際経営学研究科修了（MBA）。国際基督教大学
博士（学術）。
著書に『対訳　英語で学ぶコーポレートファイナンス入門（第2版）』，『対訳　英語で学ぶ
バリュエーション入門』，『組織を動かす経営管理』，『図解　ビジネスファイナンス（第2版）』
（以上中央経済社），『会社のものさし―実学「読む」経営指標入門』（東洋経済新報社）など。

対訳

英語で学ぶ財務会計入門

2021 年 9 月 15 日　第 1 版第 1 刷発行
2024 年 1 月 30 日　第 1 版第 2 刷発行

著　者	本　合　暁　詩	
発 行 者	山　本　　　継	
発 行 所	㈱ 中 央 経 済 社	
発 売 元	㈱中央経済グループ パブリッシング	

〒101-0051　東京都千代田区神田神保町1-35
電話 03 (3293) 3371 (編集代表)
　　 03 (3293) 3381 (営業代表)
https://www.chuokeizai.co.jp

©2021
Printed in Japan

印刷／文 唱 堂 印 刷 ㈱
製本／㈲ 井 上 製 本 所

ISBN 978-4-502-39601-4　C3034

本書とともにお薦めします

本合　暁詩 [著]

米国大学の講義内容をそのまま提供！
バイリンガルで学ぶ好評シリーズ

対訳 英語で学ぶ
コーポレート
ファイナンス入門
（第2版）

A5 判・304 頁

対訳 英語で学ぶ
バリュエーション
入門

A5 判・272 頁

中央経済社